NEXT-DAY
SALARY NEGOTIATION

prepare tonight to get your best pay tomorrow

MARYANNE WEGERBAUER
and The Editors @ JIST

Also in JIST's Help in a Hurry Series

JIST *Works*
America's Career Publisher™

PART OF JIST'S HELP IN A HURRY™ SERIES

NEXT-DAY SALARY NEGOTIATION

© 2007 by JIST Publishing, Inc.

Published by JIST Works, an imprint of JIST Publishing, Inc.
8902 Otis Avenue
Indianapolis, IN 46216-1033
Phone: 1-800-648-JIST   Fax: 1-800-JIST-FAX   E-mail: info@jist.com

Visit our Web site at www.jist.com for information on JIST, free job search tips, book chapters, and ordering instructions for our many products! For free information on 14,000 job titles, visit www.careeroink.com.

Quantity discounts are available for JIST books. Have future editions of JIST books automatically delivered to you on publication through our convenient standing order program. Please call our Sales Department at 1-800-648-5478 for a free catalog and more information.

Acquisitions and Development Editor: Lori Cates Hand
Project Editor: Jill Mazurczyk
Interior Designer: Aleata Howard
Page Layout: Trudy Coler, Lacey Duncan
Cover Designer: Katy Bodenmiller
Proofreader: Paula Lowell
Indexer: Tina Trettin

Printed in the United States of America
12 11 10 09 08 07   9 8 7 6 5 4 3 2 1

Library of Congress Cataloging-in-Publication Data

Wegerbauer, Maryanne L.
  Next-day salary negotiation : prepare tonight to get your best pay tomorrow / Maryanne Wegerbauer and the editors at JIST.
     p. cm. -- (JIST's help in a hurry series)
  Includes index.
  ISBN 978-1-59357-440-6 (alk. paper)
  1. Wages. 2. Negotiation in business. 3. Job offers. I. JIST Works, Inc. II. Title.
  HD4909.W44 2007
  650.1'2--dc22
                                        2007000650

ISBN 978-1-59357-440-6

About This Book

In the hectic pace of interviewing for jobs, you can be taken off guard when you are actually made an offer. You might be so excited by the offer that you don't take time to evaluate it, much less negotiate for higher pay and better benefits and work arrangements. Yet, studies show that 60 percent of the time, employers leave room in their first offer for some negotiation.

Instead of accepting the first offer and possibly leaving some money on the table, it pays to do your homework. This book can help you prepare for a negotiation overnight, by reading the 10 Quick and Essential Tips in chapter 1. If you have a little more time, you can go into more depth in chapters 2 through 6, which give details on researching the company, quantifying your value and negotiating power, evaluating the offer, planning and strategizing the negotiation, and employing negotiation tips and techniques.

An added bonus is the extensive salary tables in chapter 7 of this book. You can look up and cite average salary by geographic area and experience level for nearly 280 jobs that cover 80 percent of the U.S. economy.

So do yourself a favor and employ the tips and techniques in this book. For the investment of a few bucks and a couple of hours, you could walk away from your negotiation with thousands of dollars more than you were originally offered.

We wish you good fortune in your negotiations and your life.

Contents

A Brief Introduction to Using This Book

I deally, the best way to prepare for a negotiation is to research the company and the job for a week or two, get a good handle on your qualifications and experience, extensively research salary ranges, and carefully consider your response to the initial offer and subsequent counter-offers. But you have a negotiation tomorrow and have been too busy to prepare before now. How can you get up to speed tonight?

1. **Read some quick tips that will dramatically improve your performance.** The tips in chapter 1 will quickly help you improve your negotiation skills—enough for a negotiation later today or tomorrow. They provide a short but thorough course and give you the most important things to remember as you go into the negotiation.

2. **Get the inside scoop.** Chapter 2 shows you some quick ways to find information about the job and the company that will come in handy.

3. **Know yourself.** Use the worksheets in chapter 3 to quantify your value to the company, as well as your power in the negotiation.

4. **Evaluate the offer.** Chapter 4 dissects the numerous elements of a job offer and helps you decide which are most important to you.

5. **Have a plan.** Chapter 5 gives advice on planning the negotiation and implementing a strategy.

6. **Communicate effectively.** Chapter 6 explains the importance of listening well and saying the right things the right way.

7. **Have salary data at your fingertips.** Chapter 7 is an extensive listing of salary averages for nearly 280 of the most popular jobs in our economy, grouped by experience level and geographic location.

8. **Sum it up.** The appendix is a worksheet that helps you organize all of your thoughts and data, and to compare the offer to your current job or another offer.

There is no need to read these materials sequentially; just spend time where you think the biggest payoff is for you and where you need the most help. So what are you waiting for? Jump in and start improving your negotiating skills right now!

Chapter 1

Quick and Essential Tips for Tomorrow's Negotiation

C ongratulations! You've made it through several rounds of interviews and are the chosen candidate for the job. Your potential employer has either made you an offer or has asked you to come in to discuss an offer. Or you have the feeling they will soon. Whatever the scenario, it's likely you'll be facing a negotiation in the near future. This chapter identifies the top 10 most important things to know before you negotiate.

Caution: *Don't ignore the potential for damaging a newly formed relationship. Hard bargaining often creates resentment and defensiveness. Win-lose negotiating can lead to a win-lose situation for you: You get what you wanted, but you start your new job with the handicap of having caused ill will during the negotiations.*

1. Keep a Positive Attitude

How you think about and handle negotiating will greatly affect the result. Have an open mind and a positive outlook. Your expectations will communicate themselves and influence the outcome of the negotiations.

Here are some tips for approaching the negotiation in a positive way:

- View the negotiation as a forum for an exchange of ideas.

- Create a tone of cooperation and collaboration.

- Use your interpersonal skills to establish rapport and reaffirm your commitment to the company and the job.

- Stress common or aligned interests and your potential to further the organization's goals.

- Communicate your value to the employer in terms of your ability to perform the job functions.

- Keep the focus on how you can contribute to the business.

2. Time the Negotiation Properly

The timing of the actual negotiation discussion is critical. The best time to negotiate is after a serious job offer has been made and before you have fully accepted it. When an offer is extended, the employer has made the decision that you are the qualified recruit best suited for the job. You are interested, but you may still be evaluating all of the opportunities available to you. You have not yet made a commitment. It is at this point that you have the most bargaining leverage.

> **Caution:** *Avoid getting involved in discussions about salary and other components of a job offer before an actual offer is made. Doing so can harm your negotiation stance down the road, so attempt to defer these discussions until the employer makes you an offer.*

Once the employer has fully stated the terms of the offer, express interest and enthusiasm and then ask for time to consider the job offer, given the importance of the decision. This creates a brief period in which to prepare for negotiating the design of the job itself (the job description and how you will perform it), compensation and benefits, and job perks. You probably have given some preliminary thought to each of these areas, so you might already have a good general sense of what compensation and benefits you can expect and how much you really want the job.

3. Gather Necessary Information and Tools

An important part of preparing for a negotiation is to gather the essential tools that will help you in the process. Gather the following and take it with you to the negotiation meeting:

- Name, title, location, and telephone number of the party with whom you are negotiating
- Previous correspondence with that person or with company representatives
- Notes and questions
- Organizational information and materials, including an employee handbook

- Your personal marketing statement (see chapter 3)
- Copy of your resume
- Samples of your work for reference, if appropriate
- Professional recommendations
- Business cards
- Pen and notepad
- Proposed process and criteria
- Your list of negotiating priorities (see chapter 4), a loosely drafted agenda (see chapter 5), and a rough estimate of how much money the company will make or save as a result of hiring you
- Industry and profession-specific salary and benefit survey information (see chapter 7)

4. Research the Organization

In evaluating a job offer and preparing to negotiate terms of employment, it is helpful to be familiar with the organization as a business entity. To be successful in negotiations, you must adapt your strategy to fit the organization's culture and the personality of the person with whom you'll be negotiating.

Aspects of the organization with which you should become familiar are the following:

- Culture
- Structure
- Management style
- Organizational communications

Chapter 2 gives more insight as to how to gather information on these aspects of the organization before your negotiation. In general, you'll probably get the bulk of your information from speaking to current or former employees, doing research on the Internet, and following your own intuition.

5. Know Your Value and Bargaining Power

Relative power is perhaps the most critical concept of negotiations to master. Each party to the negotiation has a certain degree of strength—the ability to supply or fulfill the needs and wants of the other party. Knowing your strengths and resources, your ability to respond to the needs of the other party, and your competition enables you to more accurately assess your bargaining position in relation to that of the employer.

Factors contributing to your relative power in the negotiation include the business climate in which the company operates, the company's stability, the employer's urgency to fill the position, your own expertise (and the availability of other qualified candidates), and other options you may have, such as a current job or other offers.

It is essential to determine your relative power in the negotiation beforehand. That way, you'll have a better idea of how much you can ask for in the negotiation. Chapter 3 provides more details and a worksheet for maximizing your relative strength in the negotiation.

6. Almost Everything Is Negotiable

Although you are probably focused most acutely on the salary for the position, there are many other aspects of the total job offer that are up for negotiation. In your zeal to maximize your base pay, don't neglect to explore other terms of work that are important to you. Examples of the kinds of benefits that might be up for negotiation are the following:

- Position description and responsibilities
- Flexible work arrangements
- Paid time off
- Bonus plans
- Stock options
- Health insurance
- Dependent care
- Disability pay
- Retirement and termination provisions
- Relocation assistance
- Business and travel reimbursement
- Tuition reimbursement

Chapter 4 helps you evaluate all facets of a job offer and decide which aspects are the most important to your personally. These will be your negotiation priorities.

7. Plan the Negotiation

Planning the negotiation is about mentally setting the stage for negotiations. It is mapping out an approach, based on information you have gathered, to reach an objective.

Be well informed with both background information and thorough knowledge of the points to be discussed. Gather information about the environment in which the negotiation will occur. Know "who, what, when, where, why, and how":

- With whom you will be negotiating
- What you know about them and their personal style
- When and where the negotiations will take place
- Why you are negotiating—what you want—and how you will handle the discussions

Chapter 5 has more information on how to plan the various aspects of the negotiation.

8. Set Your Strategy

Strategy is determining the means you will use to get to the outcome you desire. Ideally, your negotiation plan is guided by a strategy for achieving your goals and objectives. Chapter 5 has detailed information on choosing and following a negotiation strategy.

9. Hone Your Communication Skills

Successful negotiators remain fully attuned to what the other party is saying, verbally and nonverbally, and how the other party is reading and reacting to their messages throughout the agreement process.

Here are some tips on interpersonal communications skills that will help you get the best outcome from the negotiation:

- **Know the audience.** Determine what you can about the personality of the individual with whom you will be negotiating and adapt your communication style to work best with theirs.
- **Start on a positive note.** Begin the negotiation with an opening statement acknowledging your mutual goals. Validate (or readjust) your

understanding of the employer's needs. Establish a climate of reason-ability and keep the interaction low key.

- **Build trust.** Underscore your agreement on aligned issues. Emphasize your expertise, competence, and ability to get things done, as well as your commitment and credibility. Convey a genuine desire to reach a fair agreement.

- **Value the relationship.** Take the long view. It is likely that you will be working with the person with whom you are negotiating. Adopting an uncompromising stance or making the negotiation competitive or adversarial would be detrimental to your future working relationship.

- **Use persuasive language.** Influence and win over the other party using a convincing, rather than coercing, communication style. Introduce a possible trade-off by first noting agreement: "If we agree that it will be necessary for me to be available on call, would you agree that some additional flex time could be incorporated into my schedule?" Compromise openings, such as "What if" or "How would you feel about" allow you to bring up topics in an exploratory form, rather than a demanding one. Be at ease, allowing reflective pauses to punctuate the discussion.

- **Use positive body language.** Meeting in person with the other party for a negotiation is much more productive than conducting the discussion over the telephone. Particularly important in the initial stages of the process, your posture, body language, and facial expressions can help you project sincerity and good will.

- **Expect conflict.** Not all conflict is negative or to be avoided. On the contrary, a certain amount of discord can be anticipated during the course of the negotiation. Expressing different views on issues serves the purpose of identifying what is really of importance to each party, a necessary stage in the process of working toward agreement.

- **Deal with resistance.** When you meet with strong resistance, proceed with caution. Remain sensitive to the other party's position. Suggest a solution that addresses their concerns, as well as your own, in order to move forward. Resistance may mean that it's time to make a small accommodation, offer to meet halfway, or take a break from the issue. Avoid the creation of an interpersonal barrier. Rather, continue to communicate with understanding and remain open to possibilities.

- **Know when to conclude.** Wrap up the negotiation graciously, without pushing for closure. Allow some time for thoughtful consideration of the terms of the agreement. If necessary, set a time to reconvene to finalize the agreement.

Chapter 6 has more details on what to say during various phases of the negotiation.

10. Determine a Fair Base Salary Range for the Position

Several factors contribute to what the job will pay, including the company's pay philosophy, national salary averages for similar jobs, and your individual experience and qualifications.

The Company's Pay Philosophy

First, try to determine the company's overall pay philosophy. Know the company's total compensation approach and the level of labor competition it faces. How a business pays its workers often reflects its position in the business life cycle; for example, a well-established company might be able to offer more cash compensation, whereas a startup business might emphasize equity (stock) opportunity. Factors that companies consider in determining salary budgets include the business plan, past financial results and future prospects, staffing strategy (the caliber of workers it wants to attract and retain), and affordability (what the employer can afford to pay).

A company's pay philosophy—whether to pay at, above, or below the market and the mix of base and variable pay—largely follows from the business mission and plan to attract employees with the knowledge, skills, and abilities required to achieve the company's objectives. In addition to researching these influences, keep in mind that many employers have a pay for performance program today. Inquiring about this in a conversational mode might open up discussion about the company's compensation philosophy and program specifics.

The Market for the Job

Have a sense of the market and what competitive pay is for similar work. Research pay for similar jobs. You can find published salary surveys in the library or on the Internet, but be sure to consider the reliability of the survey source. Surveys and polls are shaped by the sponsor, the design, the position descriptions, the company participant group, how well the positions match up, and the statistical methodology used to produce the survey results. Don't use the job title as a benchmark. The key is how closely the offered position matches the surveyed job functionally and in size and scope of responsibility.

The Bureau of Labor Statistics (BLS) surveys are one readily available source of market data. Industry and occupational surveys generally contain data that pertain more closely to specialized work environments and jobs. Chapter 7 of this book summarizes BLS average wage data for hundreds of the most common jobs in our economy (covering more than 80 percent of the workforce) and is a good point of reference.

Following are some suggested Web sites for salary research:

- bls.gov
- careerjournal.com
- cbsalary.com
- collegejournal.com
- payscale.com
- salary.com
- salaryexpert.com

Your Experience and Qualifications

Obviously, the more experience and talent you bring to the position, the higher base salary you will be able to command. To some extent, the existing job was shaped by the person who performed it before you. Recognize the value that your knowledge, skills, and abilities will contribute—will you be able to offer as much or more than the previous employee? On the other hand, acknowledge that a career change, a location change, or an opportunity for learning may be worth more to you than a high beginning salary figure.

Key Points: Chapter 1

- Approach the negotiation with a positive, collaborative attitude.
- Negotiate after a firm offer has been made and before you have accepted it.
- Gather necessary tools to take with you to the negotiation.
- Research the organization and be familiar with its culture, structure, management philosophy, and more.
- Know your relative power in the negotiation.
- Be prepared to negotiate other parts of the total job offer.
- Plan the negotiation and set your strategy in advance.
- Use active listening and collaborative language during the negotiation.
- Know the salary range for the position.

Chapter 2

Research the Organization

I n preparation for interviews, you probably collected information on the organization. Look back again at the business environment within which the employer operates. A trip online or to the library will yield a wealth of resource materials—directories, references, business magazines, and newspapers. Research the employer through trade publications. Review the company's annual report, 10K report (filed with the Securities and Exchange Commission), and proxy statements. Request and read a comprehensive benefits booklet from the employer.

Think about the negotiation from the employer's point of view. Identify the employer's probable issues, gauge the employer's position, and anticipate the employer's arguments. Then, research and be able to articulate the implications of the issues from a business, as well as a human, perspective. Script your proposals, practice responding verbally with a tape recorder, or even use videotape to perfect your presentation.

Four main aspects of the organization that you should research and seek to understand are its culture, its structure, its management style, and the way it communicates with its employees, as well as the public. These characteristics influence how able the company will be to meet your needs—both in the negotiation and as an employee.

Researching Organizational Culture

People often identify with an organization most strongly through its culture. Culture is the backdrop for the work performed in an organization. It sets the course—formal or informal, isolated or supportive, risk-averse or entrepreneurial—of the organization.

Organizational culture is a complexity that develops around "the way we do things" within a company. Essentially, it is the nature and identity of an organization. Culture is made up of taken-for-granted assumptions, expectations, and sometimes, misconceptions. It is made up of an organization's shared values and meanings, exhibited through ways of doing the work of the business. A company's culture is a central set of beliefs that provide the rationale for a particular view and orientation toward work and ways of behaving within the organization.

The company's geographic location, its presence in the community, union or nonunion status, and any special interests contribute to the definition of its culture. Indicators of the culture include the degree of flexibility the organization offers. Individual and group demographics, such as the mix between younger and older employees, singles and married people (with or without children), may be representative of the culture. The professional-technical-clerical composition, length of time workers have been with the company, and overall level of employee education are factors contributing to the company's workforce profile.

To some extent, organizational culture is an indicator of which parts of the job offer may or may not be negotiable. For example, in discussing work arrangements at an organization known for routinely long workdays, expressing an interest in a flexible schedule might be negatively viewed as indicating a lack of commitment to the job. (The cultural "schedule" may be to come in early and work late.)

Before evaluating and negotiating the offer, look once more at the organization itself. Is the organization's philosophy and culture a comfortable operating climate for you? How should you adapt your negotiating strategy to fit its culture?

Take a Look Around

You can tell a lot about an organization just by looking around outside at the buildings, grounds, landscaping and maintenance, and parking. As you observe the organization's facility, ask yourself questions such as these:

- Inside, are visitors welcomed and made comfortable in a reception area?
- Within the corridors and work areas, what is the level of activity? Is it quiet or noisy?
- How is the workspace designed? Is it well appointed, well equipped, and well lit?
- What is the style of office furniture and decor? Does it look modern and trendy, or does it show signs of neglect?
- Are the materials, tools, and resources you need to do your work readily available?
- Do people wear business attire or dress casually?
- Is there a smoking policy?
- Are there other observable social or behavioral standards?

- How does this organization compare with others in the same industry or field?

Read the Company Literature

Companies often explain their organizational philosophy in their corporate vision, their values commitment (which states "how we work"), or the corporate mission statement (which states "why we work").

If your interviewer did not give you copies of the corporate mission statement and other company literature, you can often find these on the organization's Web site. If not, you can call the human resources or public relations department and ask for a copy. If these materials do not exist, that's a clue in and of itself: The corporate culture may be too informal, or the company too small, for management to have spent time producing these materials.

After you have read the mission statement and other materials, ask yourself whether this philosophy will accommodate your values and personal work environment preferences—your employment likes and dislikes. If not, you may lean toward declining the job offer.

Researching Organizational Structure

The structure of an organization and the way it makes decisions will directly bias what might be negotiable and with whom you must undertake the negotiations in order for them to be productive.

The structure of an organization includes the ways in which people are grouped to perform work. Traditional organizations often cluster workers based on profession and tenure. Many organizations now have interdisciplinary, cross-functional, or process teams focused on putting out a quality product efficiently or implementing cost savings. Startup venture and network organizations may essentially have one group of employees who work together on phased implementations, motivated by profit-sharing incentives.

Organizational structure is the set upon which work is performed. It shapes the way work is performed, prescribes job definition to some extent, and affects the significance of interdepartmental worker relationships. A traditional structure may indicate clearly defined job duties, with little room for alternative design; whereas in a matrixed organization (in which an employee can report to more than one manager), job content is more likely to be continually adapting.

A company's latitude to negotiate employment terms varies. Smaller companies may have fewer rules and regulations but may be correspondingly less familiar with possibilities. Larger, more bureaucratic organizations may be less flexible because they require more approvals from more people before decisions can be made. Unionized environments are highly structured and usually have little if any tolerance for individually negotiated situations. Be sure to understand what specific conditions and constraints exist that might impact the negotiation.

Researching Management Style

A good grasp of the management style of both the company and the manager will help you plan your negotiation strategy. A company's management practices are a significant factor in whether you would be comfortable and successful working there. Individual work performance and satisfaction are strongly influenced by a manager's style, coaching, and communications skills. Management preferences set the tone of the immediate environment within which a position functions.

Company Management Style

If a company's management is centralized or highly controlling, you will need to approach negotiations cautiously. Your strategy here might be to pay your respects to the organization's authoritative management style up front and acknowledge that this might make it more difficult initially to identify areas of flexibility. If the management of an organization is team-oriented, on the other hand, a negotiating strategy emphasizing openness and communications might be most productive.

Individual Management Style

A manager's particular problem-solving preferences—whether action- and results-focused, theoretical and forward thinking, cautious and thoughtful, or cooperative and concerned for others—reflect the management style with which an employee will most closely interact. Through self-assessment and experience, you will have become acquainted with your own inclinations and know whether you work best with a relatively high emphasis on task and accomplishment, or in an environment geared more toward teamwork, where relationships carry relatively greater weight.

Gaining insight into management style can help you decide whether you can work comfortably with an individual. Style assessment also provides information for choosing your approach to the job-offer negotiation.

A number of indicators can help you identify a manager's values and preferred way of working. You can infer management style from the relative value a person places on task accomplishment and relationship maintenance and how an individual frames his or her conversations, as well as from references relative to their general work outlook and focus (see the following grid).

Perspective-Focus Grid

Sensing	Intuiting
Outlook Present	*Outlook Future*
Focus: immediate action	Focus: long-range, big picture
Style: challenge-oriented, problem-solving	Style: conceptual, theoretical
Thinking	**Feeling**
Outlook Progression	*Outlook Past*
Focus: organization and analysis	Focus: relationships
Style: logical, systematic	Style: empathetic, cooperative, conventional

The style analysis shown here is based on preference identification theory developed by Carl Jung, as interpreted, adapted, and popularized by Myers-Briggs and others. It is meaningful in that we all have our own way of viewing work and work focus, preferences that fall somewhere within and between the four quadrants, some of which are more compatible with specific management styles than others.

Do you know where your own work style would be plotted on the perspective-focus grid? How does each operating style outlined in the grid fit with your own view of work?

Another way to identify management preference is simply to ask questions and evaluate the answers during the interview process. This is the most practical method for a job seeker attempting to evaluate the management style of a potential employer. Sample questions might be the following:

- What is your approach to management?
- What work style do you look for in members of your team?

- How do you ensure achievement of your objectives?
- How do you handle a crisis?
- How do you view work/family issues?
- What is the turnover experience here and why is this position open?
- How, and how often, do you communicate with your staff?
- How, and how often, do you provide performance feedback to your staff?
- What work-related qualities do you most value in your staff?

Look for open and honest replies, ask for examples or clarification if necessary, and read the manager's body language.

Researching Organizational Communication

Like management style, organizational communications offer significant clues to a company's personality. Is communication top-down and dictatorial, or bottom-up and strongly influenced by employees? Does centralized communication take place in a "stovepipe"—one-way down and/or up? Or is communication decentralized, occurring across a web—between suborganizational business units and disciplines and freely among individuals at all levels?

The way in which your job offer is communicated—whether it is made in person, conveyed over the telephone, or confirmed in writing—may be an indication of a company's communications practices. If the offer is formal, carefully worded, and crisp (brisk, matter-of-fact, and to the point), its terms are likely to be fairly rigid. If the offer is presented in a more casual manner initially, inviting discussion, there may be more room for negotiation.

Are you comfortable in a structured setting, knowing basically "what to do and how to do it," and working with information provided on a need-to-know basis? Or do you prefer to see the larger picture and the interconnection of the elements of business? Do you view knowledge and information as part of your power base, or do you openly and readily share your knowledge and expertise with others? The communication network of an organization is an observable phenomenon, representative of the atmosphere in which you will work.

ORGANIZATIONAL RESEARCH WORKSHEET

Use the following checklist to guide your research or to review and add to the information about the company that you gathered in preparation for earlier interviews.

Business Environment and Organization Characteristics

- Climate of the external operating environment (overall economy, legislation, and regulations affecting the business)
- Industry trends and competitors
- Reputation in industry
- Financial history
- Business milestones
- Annual report
- Revenues
- Primary functions
- Size
- Products, processes, equipment, and resources

Corporate Culture, Structure, and Management Style

- History
- Philosophy and culture
- General short- and long-term business goals
- Centralized/decentralized organizational configuration
- Location(s)
- Formal/informal makeup and style of management
- Communications channels
- Key names, titles

Key Points: Chapter 2

- An organization's culture provides a cue for assessing your fit within the organization and what components of the job offer may be negotiable.

- An organization's structure is often an indication of its flexibility, and as such it will have a direct bearing on the negotiation process.

- You must take management practice into consideration when planning your negotiation strategy.

- Communication practices are a visible indicator of an employer's culture, structure, and style of management.

Chapter 3

Know Your Value and Negotiating Power

Before negotiating salary, you must have a clear idea of your value to the company, as well as other advantages you might have in the negotiation. This chapter helps you assess your worth and determine how much power you will have to negotiate a more favorable work arrangement and higher salary.

Assessing Your Value to the Company

Knowing yourself and recognizing the added value you bring to the organization in the form of knowledge, skills, abilities, experience, and education is important. If you are going to ask the employer for more money, better benefits, and a flexible work schedule, for example, you have to be able to show them what they will get in return: a loyal, experienced employee who will contribute directly to the bottom line.

Competitive Advantage Summary

Use the following worksheet to review and summarize the combination of specialized knowledge, skills, abilities, experience, and accomplishments that made you the standout candidate for the job. Look over your resume for specific strengths to emphasize during the negotiation, and try to recall the accomplishments that impressed the interviewer the most. These will form the solid foundation of added value upon which you can build your negotiation strategy.

COMPETITIVE ADVANTAGE WORKSHEET

Knowledge

_____

_____

_____

_____

_____

_____

_____

_____

_____

_____

Skills

_____

_____

_____

_____

_____

_____

_____

_____

_____

_____

_____

Abilities/Talents

_____

_____

_____

_____

_____

_____

_____

_____

_____

_____

Experience

_____

_____

_____

_____

_____

_____

_____

_____

_____

_____

_____

_____

(continued)

(continued)

Accomplishments

_____

_____

_____

_____

_____

_____

_____

_____

_____

_____

Education

_____

_____

_____

_____

_____

_____

_____

_____

Personal Marketing Statement

Using the Competitive Advantage Worksheet in the preceding section, create a summary of your experience, knowledge, skills, and abilities now, using the following worksheet as an example. Always keep in mind where you would like to be three to five years down the road.

PERSONAL MARKETING EXAMPLE

Interpersonal or background note: _____
_____
_____.

Product/Services (What I Am)

I am an experienced _____ (occupation)
with expertise in _____ (area[s] of
focus) and/or I have a degree in _____
(educational background).

Work History/Environment

Most recently I_____
_____
_____
_____
(major accomplishment, quantified in terms of numbers).

Skills (What I Do—People, Data, Things)

My strengths include _____
_____
_____
_____ (specific skills).

Traits/Interpersonal Linkage (Who I Am—Characteristics)

My areas of interest are _____
_____
_____
_____.

Goals (What I Want)

My goals include _____
_____
_____.

Determining Your Relative Power in the Negotiation

Relative power is perhaps the most critical concept of negotiations to master. Each party to the negotiation has a certain degree of strength—the ability to supply or fulfill the needs and wants of the other party. Knowing your strengths and resources, your ability to respond to the needs of the other party, and your competition enables you to more accurately assess your bargaining position in relation to that of the other person.

Relative power is the degree of influence each party has on the outcome of a negotiation. It is essentially a function of supply and demand. Relative power is directly related to the number and desirability of the other options available to each party. In other words, if there are many qualified candidates for the position, the company probably has more relative power than you do. If you have several job offers on the table at one time, you are the one with the power.

Factors Contributing to Your Relative Power

Factors contributing to the relative power of both employer and employee in designing work agreements include the following:

Business Climate

- **The state of the economy and the industry:** A healthy company will be more eager to hire than one that is struggling.

- **The overall unemployment rate and the general employment picture:** When many people are clamoring for few positions, the company has no incentive to be flexible in negotiations.

- **The demand for industry- and profession-specific knowledge and skills:** If there is a shortage of people who can do the job, employers are likely to offer better salaries and benefits, and be more flexible in negotiating them.

Company

- **Profitability:** A profitable company has more spare cash to spend on hiring new people.

- **The employing company's place in the business cycle:** Start-up, growing/new market, stable/profitable, and underperforming/

turnaround organizations all have different levels of hiring flexibility and staffing needs.

Hiring Manager

- **Urgency of the business's need to fill the position:** If the company is losing money every day the job is not filled, they will be more willing to pay top dollar to get the right candidate on the job as soon as possible.

- **Decision-making authority:** If the person you interview with must get approval from several layers of management for every request you make in the negotiations, it will take longer and you will be less likely to get what you ask for.

- **Staffing budget:** If the department has a limited amount it can spend on salaries, your request for more money likely can't be honored.

Individual

- **Availability of other opportunities:** If you are currently employed or have another offer in the wings, you are in a better negotiating position.

- **Technical expertise, unique knowledge/skill set:** If you have rare expertise that's in demand, employers will be more willing to pay more to get you.

- **Resources (financial depth, networks, and so on):** If you can afford not to take the job, you can hold out for a better offer.

- **Level of competition/availability of other candidates for the position:** If many people are interested in and qualified for the job, the company is not likely to be flexible in negotiations.

- **Career risk:** If this job is not exactly aligned with your future career goals, it should take more money to persuade you to take a chance on it.

Assess Your Relative Power

Use the following worksheet to assess the employer's circumstances and flexibility in relation to your own opportunities, unique skills, and resources; the competition; and your career objectives.

In the Negotiable Element section, list a component of the job offer. For Business Climate, consider factors such as the economy, the industry, the unemployment rate, and the demand for skills and knowledge. For Your

Relative Power, consider the other opportunities available to you, your own unique skills and knowledge, your competition for the job, and how the job fits into your overall career goals. For Employer Flexibility, consider the company's profitability and place in the business cycle, its urgency to fill the position, and the decision-making authority and staffing budget of the person with whom you are negotiating. For Notes, list your other thoughts and observations.

RELATIVE POWER WORKSHEET

Negotiable Element: _____

Business Climate: _____

Your Relative Power: _____

Employer Flexibility: _____

Notes: _____

Negotiable Element: _____

Business Climate: _____

Your Relative Power: _____

Employer Flexibility: _____

Notes: _____

Negotiable Element: _____

_____

Business Climate: _____

_____

Your Relative Power: _____

_____

Employer Flexibility: _____

_____

Notes: _____

_____

Negotiable Element: _____

_____

Business Climate: _____

_____

Your Relative Power: _____

_____

Employer Flexibility: _____

_____

Notes: _____

_____

Key Points: Chapter 3

- Know your value to the company and be prepared to favorably reference your skills set and abilities during negotiations.
- Negotiating power is directly related to the number and desirability of the other options available to each party.

Chapter 4

Evaluate the Offer

A job offer is made up of many more components than just salary. Being familiar with the different elements of an offer and knowing which are most important to you is excellent preparation for going into a negotiation.

This chapter gives details on the main components of the typical job offer, including job design, compensation, and benefits. Along the way, you'll find worksheets for evaluating the components and measuring the offer against your current situation or a second offer.

Job Design

Matching a candidate with a job is a joint venture involving both the applicant and the potential employer. Each has interests at stake and wants the relationship to be successful. An early part of the negotiation is the process of presenting, discussing, and agreeing upon the job objectives and how an individual's skills and abilities will be used in the workplace.

Work functions—what you will be doing in the organization, and how— are no longer set in stone. The design of a job could be negotiable. Rapidly changing jobs create a need for ongoing learning. With this fundamental change comes an opportunity to enhance your job satisfaction by reexamining job design.

Tips on Evaluating Job Design

Clarify the position, obtaining as much information about the job as possible. If a position description is not available, write an acceptable one. Keep in mind that job descriptions should summarize the most important functions of a job and not become a long list of tasks performed in support of job functions. Nail down the design and content of the job before you accept the offer by asking the right questions.

Here's where your research from earlier chapters will be helpful. Review your work strengths and weaknesses, likes and dislikes. Then look at the organizational culture, vision, and values (see chapter 3). Is it structured or open? Formal or casual? If you haven't already done so, ask for a tour of the facility and the department where you will be working. What is the management style? How is performance measured and evaluated? Consider the risk and reward/recognition opportunity.

Take into account the business environment. Where is the organization in its business life cycle? What is its future direction? Align your job design and job content proposals with the company's direction and strategic planning. Know the company's business model and financial picture. What is the specific added value of the position in supporting employer goals? What is the unique added value that you bring to the position?

Define the Position and See How Well It Fits You

The following worksheet will help you define the position and analyze how well it fits you. Does the open position make the most of your strengths and give you the opportunity to continue your career growth? Review your resume and identify specific areas of job design, job content, and control over work that you want to address during negotiations.

JOB DESIGN WORKSHEET

Context

Industry trends and growth prospects: _____

_____

_____

Organizational Structure

Senior management/company goals: _____

_____

_____

Partnerships and alliances:_____

_____

_____

Markets/new markets and products/new products: _____

_____

_____

Management style/tolerance for innovation: _____

_____

_____

Organizational reporting/matrixed relationships: _____

_____

_____

Work flow: _____

_____

_____

Span of control:_____

_____

_____

Scope of authority and discretion, and decision-making responsibilities: _____

_____

_____

Job Accountabilities/Objectives/Deliverables

Short-term and long-term department goals: _____

_____

_____

Client/customer base: _____

_____

_____

(continued)

(continued)

Job functions: _____

_____

Immediate problems/priorities and most important contribution:

_____

_____

Resources

Information distribution/communication loops: _____

_____

_____

People (staff), number and qualifications, administrative support:

_____

_____

Technology: _____

_____

_____

Budget: _____

_____

_____

Time: _____

_____

_____

Risk and Reward

Performance appraisal system, measures, review timetable and standards: _____

_____

_____

Rewards/recognition:_____

_____

_____

Development

Career path flexibility/progression: _____

_____

_____

Professional growth: _____

_____

_____

Accoutrements

Title: _____

_____

Status/Organizational Recognition: _____

Perks: _____

_____

Cash Compensation

Compensation is an appropriately equivalent payment in exchange for the work performed. Cash compensation is made up of the base pay and any variable pay, such as bonuses and other incentives.

You don't have to become an expert in compensation and benefits to negotiate a job offer; you simply need to get acquainted with what the questions are. To evaluate a compensation package, ask yourself the following:

- What is the relevance of each of the elements in the package?
- How does each component affect you?
- What is the implication of the whole package in relationship to who you are and what you want to accomplish?

- Will the position reward you in proportion to your expected contribution?

- Will you have the opportunity to advance professionally and increase your compensation through periodic reassessment of your base salary and bonus opportunity?

- How will performance be factored into the picture?

Consider the value of the total compensation package that the employer is offering. The prospect of a 10 percent increase in total compensation usually indicates that a job change is worthwhile.

Base Salary

Base salary is compensation as an annual, monthly, biweekly, or weekly dollar amount, usually fixed for a period of time. Hourly base pay is the rate of pay per hour for the job being performed.

> **Tip:** *Talk to your accountant or refer to applicable Internal Revenue Service publications to assess the tax implications of the offer package.*

How Employers Set Salary Ranges

A base salary range represents what the company is willing to pay for the job functions. A salary range may be determined by an internal formula or by the cost of labor—competitive pay for similar or benchmark jobs in the external marketplace—or by a combination. An organization's compensation strategy can also be influenced by that of other companies in the industry. Many companies participate in compensation surveys and use the results to assess competitive pay. Benchmark jobs, used for comparison, are sets of defined work functions that are readily recognizable in or across industries.

In an organization with a salary range structure, the salary you are offered is arrived at by reviewing the position's salary range; your individual experience, knowledge, and skills; and usually, the market price—how much people are making in similar jobs in other companies, as well as the salaries of current employees doing similar work. Typically, employee pay is clustered around the midpoint, with newly hired, inexperienced employees paid lower in the range and those with significant experience or premium skills paid higher in the range.

Many factors can affect the amount of the base salary and how it is paid. Shift differential, per diem, and special schedule adjustments may be made to the base salary. If the job requires you to be on call (accessible during some period of time when you are not scheduled for work), there may be a premium or formula for additional pay for when you are called in to work.

Some companies pay employees a "retainer" or stipend, or allow them to draw a loan against their anticipated commission. Those working overseas are typically granted an expatriate allowance premium and may be eligible for special tax considerations.

Beginning Salary Discussions

When beginning salary discussions with your potential employer, never reveal your salary requirements too soon. The employer might have a higher figure in mind, but if the salary you name is lower, that's what you'll be stuck with. An employer with a lower figure in mind might rule out your candidacy prematurely, considering you unaffordable or too demanding. Instead, be prepared to respond to a preliminary inquiry with a range estimate and ask for more information about all aspects of the job's compensation.

Have a pragmatic idea of what you need to earn and be sure to get a clear understanding of what you will have to do to increase your future base pay in the job.

Assessing a Base Pay Offer

In assessing the base salary offer, first determine the company's overall pay philosophy. Know the company's total compensation approach and the level of labor competition it faces. How a business pays its workers often reflects its position in the business life cycle; for example, a well-established company may be able to offer more cash compensation, while a startup business may emphasize equity (stock) opportunity. Factors that companies consider in determining salary budgets include the business plan, past financial results and future prospects, staffing strategy—the caliber of workers it wants to attract and retain—and affordability—what the employer can afford to pay.

Have a sense of the market and what competitive pay is for similar work. Research pay for similar jobs. You can find published salary surveys in the library or on the Internet, but be sure to consider the reliability of the survey source. Surveys and polls are shaped by the sponsor, the design, the position descriptions, the company participant group, how well the reported positions are matched to the survey, and the statistical methodology that is used. Don't use the job title as a benchmark. The key is how closely the offered position matches the surveyed job functionally and in size and scope of responsibility.

The Bureau of Labor Statistics (BLS) surveys are one readily available source of market data (see chapter 7 of this book). Industry and occupational surveys generally contain data that pertain more closely to specialized work environments and jobs.

Employment firms and employment specialists may be of help in judging market demand and whether certain skills could be worth a premium. Business and trade publications, newspaper employment ads and articles, and people you know in the industry are all potential sources of information. Evaluate the available information realistically.

Variable-pay programs and annual cash bonus plans in effect also play an important part in evaluating the base pay portion of total compensation. Find out what criteria determine whether you will receive a bonus, and how the amount is arrived at.

> **Tip:** *Base salary is often the primary focus of an applicant, but it is not the only factor in considering compensation. In addition to salary, a hiring bonus, sometimes arrived at via a formula such as a percent of base salary, may be placed on the table. If the initial base-salary offer seems low, explore the possibility of a sign-on bonus.*

In addition to bonus opportunity, determine how often salary is reviewed for increase. A six-month, rather than an annual or 18-month, review cycle can provide exponentially greater possibility for future base salary increases.

Understand the job and the reporting relationships. If possible, inquire discreetly about the average range of compensation for individuals in similar jobs and in jobs at the same organizational level. To some extent, the existing job was shaped by the person who performed it before you. Recognize the value that your knowledge, skills, and abilities will contribute. Will you be able to offer as much or more than the previous employee? On the other hand, acknowledge that a career change, a location change, or an opportunity for learning may be worth more to you than a high salary.

Your bargaining power is greatest prior to accepting an offer. So don't settle for a lower base salary than you need and then hope to find ways to improve it later. Negotiate up front for the salary you want and need. Other benefits, such as disability payments and life insurance amounts, can be driven by the base salary level, so it pays to make the best deal you can.

Variable Pay: Bonuses, Profit-Sharing, and Stock Options

> **Note:** *Some companies even allow employees to take a base salary increase as a lump-sum advance, awarding a periodic increase amount as a loan up front, which the employee repays through deduction at a relatively low interest rate over the year.*

Variable pay is compensation, either cash or stock (equity) that is based on the performance of the company, a group, or an individual employee. It is a one-time payment that is not added to base pay and varies according to performance results. Variable pay is generally contingent upon the accomplishment of a predetermined goal or objective.

Variable pay opportunity allows you to more directly affect your total earnings through your performance. In assessing a job offer, it's important to have a clear understanding of the company's variable-pay programs, plan eligibility, bonus opportunity, and performance criteria.

Organization-Wide or Group Plans

Different types of group plans include the following:

- **Profit-sharing plans:** Emphasize overall company performance and generally are based on financial results. The percentage you are eligible for may be proportionate to your ability to affect the bottom line. Profit-sharing plans may be either short-term or long-term, based on the timing of distributions. If all or a portion of the profit-share funds are held inaccessible in a vested account, you may get the payout as part of a pension plan.

- **Gainsharing plans:** Measure the value of productivity and allocate shares between the employer and employees. Such plans are usually formula-based, measuring increases in productivity and profitability through cost containment and quality enhancement. Gainsharing encourages teamwork and employee commitment by making your monetary gains dependent on your impact on the company's performance.

- **Large- or small-group financial incentives:** Often flat dollar amounts divided equally among group members upon successful performance and achievement of goals. Alternatively, the payout figure can be a percentage of salary. Incentives may be tied to either department or group results and are usually determined by the degree to which the work functions influence overall results. Team-based rewards recognize the interdependency of related tasks and the amount of interaction required in accomplishing the objective.

Individual Short-Term Incentives

Individual incentive programs encourage high performance. They can take the following forms:

- Annual bonus plans
- Commissions
- Sign-on bonuses
- Awards for performance or achievement
- Spontaneous "spot" (small cash or symbolic) awards
- Gifts, such as for an employment anniversary or a national or local holiday remembrance
- Company announcements and presentations
- Noncash recognition programs, such as gift or dinner certificates, or special perks
- Travel and vacation incentives

Although you usually cannot negotiate items such as these, knowing whether a company offers them can be a factor in your evaluation of the job offer.

Long-Term Incentives

Long-term incentives, which generally have a plan term of more than one year, take the form of both capital (cash) plans and equity (stock ownership) programs. These programs are intended to link employee gain to that of the company. Long-term cash incentives include various performance unit plans.

Incentives may be "a piece of the pie" in the form of stock ownership. Programs include incentive stock options, certain stock grant and stock purchase plans, and loans to purchase stock.

When negotiating total compensation, stock options and stock ownership offer great opportunity for bridging the gap between the offered cash compensation and the desired total compensation. Often, an employer who is unwilling or unable to meet your salary expectations will be open to a discussion of incorporating stock arrangements as part of the employment offer.

Understand the program basis, timing, vesting eligibility, measurement criteria, and opportunity. Long-term financial incentives work for both the employer and employee, creating a mutual interest in the company's long-term financial success.

Evaluating Cash Compensation

Use the following worksheet to think through the total compensation makeup of the job offer. For variable-pay opportunity, consider eligibility and vesting rules, funding, award formulas, performance criteria and measurements, payment schedules, and in the case of stock incentives, exercise rights and restrictions.

BASE SALARY AND INCENTIVE WORKSHEET

Base Salary _____

Your relative power: _____

_____

Employer flexibility: _____

_____

Notes: _____

_____

Review Cycle _____

Your relative power: _____

_____

Employer flexibility: _____

_____

Notes: _____

_____

(continued)

(continued)

Equity Ownership/Stock Options

Your relative power: _____

_____

Employer flexibility: _____

_____

Notes: _____

_____

Short-Term Cash Incentive

Your relative power: _____

_____

Employer flexibility: _____

_____

Notes: _____

_____

Long-Term Incentives

Your relative power: _____

_____

Employer flexibility: _____

_____

Notes: _____

_____

Primary Employee Benefits

Most employers provide workers with a number of benefits in addition
to salary and wages. The breadth and depth of options offered vary by
company. Many companies can make different arrangements to meet
different needs; a menu of benefits allows you to choose and therefore more
closely satisfy your individual needs. Common employee benefits include
health-care insurance, income protection, and retirement funding.

Health-Care Insurance

Medical benefits are a highly desirable—and therefore highly visible—benefit. It is customary for employers to offer a fixed choice of plans and levels of coverage; negotiation opportunity is usually greatest for programs that address wellness and returning to work after an illness.

Considerations in evaluating a medical plan can include the following:

- Does the plan insure children, stepchildren, grandchildren, domestic partners, or dependent parents?
- Are there stay-duration limits in alternative-care facilities?
- What cost-containment provisions—such as hospital preadmission certification or testing, care monitoring and discharge and post-discharge planning, and insurance limitations—are in place?
- Is hospice care covered?
- Is there a lifetime benefit maximum?
- Will I have the right to convert my coverage to a private policy upon leaving the company?

You should also view medical plan protection in conjunction with a company's sick leave and disability plans—eligibility, waiting period requirements, pay amount and duration, and accumulation rules.

Comparing Medical Plans

Use the following worksheet to evaluate the medical plan(s) offered by the employer at the time of the negotiation. You can use it again after you're hired to chart in detail the types and levels of coverage you need.

MEDICAL PLAN ANALYSIS WORKSHEET
PLAN ELEMENTS
Plan: Provider and plan type/coverage level
Premium: Monthly cost to employee after flex credit
Membership: Eligibility guidelines/qualifying events

(continued)

(continued)

Costs: Noncovered costs/copay/deductible/coinsurance: Individual/dependents, maximum out-of-pocket/major medical trigger/plan maximum

Coverage: Type and percent of expenses covered: Physicians, specialists, in-patient hospital, out-patient hospital, mental health facility/rehab, dental, vision, hearing, prescription drugs, alternative care, wellness, emergency room/urgent care, radiology and lab, durable medical equipment, other

Exclusions: Coverage limits and exclusions

Plan A: _____

_____

_____

_____

_____

_____

_____

_____

_____

_____

_____

_____

_____

_____

_____

_____

Plan B: _____

_____

_____

_____

_____

Plan C: _____

Income Protection and Replacement

Income protection and income replacement plans are forms of insurance and savings that allow workers to anticipate and proactively arrange for potentially large out-of-pocket expenditures and the continuation of living expenses under adverse conditions. These benefits assist employees in planning for standard-of-living maintenance and providing for large and/or final expenses.

Loss of income could create a dramatic change in your security and standard of living. Having the opportunity to participate in income-protection programs can increase your peace of mind, contribute to your satisfaction with your new job, raise your morale, and make you more productive. With this in mind, you can point out reasonable need and mutual gain when negotiating for income protection.

You probably won't have much flexibility to negotiate income protection benefits, however. Generally, the plans and plan features offered by an employer are controlled and you need only choose whether to participate and at what level. But you should always ask questions, such as the following:

- What are the restrictions in the accidental death and dismemberment plan?
- Can you purchase in-effect, split-dollar life insurance if you leave the company?
- Are there age-related coverage reductions to employer-sponsored life insurance upon retirement?
- Is the survivor income benefit structured as a tax-free death benefit?

Disability Benefits

Short-term and long-term disability benefits are usually administered by a formula based on a percent of salary replacement. The plan will define eligibility, waiting period (if any), number of days earned or granted per specified period, term duration at 100 percent salary replacement and/or at reduced benefits, and coordination with sick days, Workers' Compensation, and Social Security benefits. Plan provisions may include continuation of service credit, savings/profit sharing credit accrual, and maintenance of health coverage during the period that you are receiving disability benefits.

Long-Term-Care Insurance

People are living longer today and families are often less able to care for relatives who need assistance with the functions of daily living. Long-term-care insurance covers very specific maintenance care, at home or in a nursing or day-care facility, in the event of an incapacitating illness. Coverage for a spouse and even for parents may also be offered, sometimes independent of employee enrollment.

Life Insurance

Life insurance is a frequently offered employment benefit, usually in the form of basic term life. There may or may not be a cost to you and the possibility of conversion when you leave the company. Additional life insurance may also be offered, where you bear the entire cost of the expanded coverage voluntarily.

Among the many forms of life insurance found in the workplace are the following:

- **Universal life:** Contains an investment element through which a cash value is accumulated; the employee generally pays the premiums.
- **Split-dollar life:** An arrangement in which the employer and employee share the expenses of the insurance and may also share in the equity and death benefits of the coverage.
- **Accidental death and dismemberment:** Provides a benefit if an accident occurs that causes death or other covered losses to the insured.
- **Business travel:** Pays survivors if the employee dies while traveling for work.
- **Dependent life insurance and survivor income benefit insurance (SIBI):** Can be arranged as either a lump sum or periodic payments to the beneficiary.

Evaluating Income Protection and Replacement Plans

Use the following worksheet to review the income-protection and replacement plans offered by the company. Are benefits continued during a period of extended illness? What are the tax implications of the benefits offered? Consider whether it would be wise to look into obtaining or supplementing any of these coverages independently.

INCOME PROTECTION AND REPLACEMENT WORKSHEET				
Benefit Feature	Priority Item (✓)	Relative Power/ Options	Employer Flexibility	Notes
Sick pay				
Short-term disability				
Long-term disability				
Long-term health care				
Life insurance forms and coverages				
Supplemental and misc. coverages				
Outside sources of income protection and replacement				

Retirement and Termination of Employment

Retirement used to be something companies designed on behalf of long-term employees. Today, retirement planning is the responsibility of the individual, working in partnership with the employer. Know the cash value of any present pension benefit in preparation for new job offer negotiations.

Find out the employing organization's pension plan type, formula, and the definition of covered pay. Clarifying questions to ask, depending on the nature of the plan, might include the following:

- Is the plan insured?
- What is the vesting convention?
- What is the normal retirement age?
- Are bonus awards included in pension payout calculations?
- Does the plan offer investment choices?
- What are the plan restrictions around investments?
- Is the 401(k) match determined by company performance? If so, how is performance measured?
- Is the savings plan account forfeited under any circumstances?
- What happens to benefits when an employee retires?
- Is there an early-retirement subsidy?
- Is there a Social Security integration in the pension determination?
- Is there a cost-of-living adjustment built into the retirement plan?

Negotiate for immediate or accelerated vesting of pension rights. Older, experienced workers may also be able to negotiate for additional years of service and/or age for pension calculations. Sometimes, an annuity can make up the difference if you lose pension benefits when changing jobs.

In the case of involuntary termination, is there a severance program or a combination salary continuation or call-back period and severance plan? Other negotiables include additional weeks of severance pay and an extension of benefits coverage and payment periods. Is there a benefits buy-back option in the event of rehire?

In instances of both voluntary and involuntary termination, a clear understanding of applicable trade secrets agreements, confidentiality, and other restrictions is essential. You may be required to sign confidentiality and/or noncompete agreements that could keep you from taking another job in the same industry for a period of time.

Additional Employee Benefits

In addition to financial compensation, health insurance, income protection, and retirement, many employers have put other benefits in place to further provide for the well-being of their workforce. Additional employee benefits include relocation support, work and family programs, and executive and supplemental benefits. Although not technically in the benefits family, travel and business expense policies are close cousins of benefits in that they are part of the company work environment standard.

Relocation Assistance

The availability of relocation assistance enables you to expand your job search geographically by making the transition to a different city easier. Often your first concern is moving and setting up a functioning household; this is a sizeable up-front expense, as well as a major investment of time. Good relocation programs alleviate much of the worry and burden of moving, freeing you to concentrate on your job with minimal disruption. Relocation support can also ease the emotional stress of family members who must deal with new schools, new friends, and a new community. Your spouse may benefit correspondingly from area-specific job search assistance, which some companies provide in order to make your whole family comfortable with the move decision.

Research the current home sales market and the cost of living in the proposed location before negotiations take place. A real estate agent who specializes in relocation can help you gather pertinent information, or you can do your own research via the Internet with tools such as the Salary Calculator at www.homefair.com. A higher cost of living in another part of the country may affect your standard of living and home-buying power considerably.

During negotiations, ask the employer for a written summary of which moving expenses will be covered. Also ask about reimbursement limits. If the company uses a generic or standard statement of policy for relocation, be sure to expand on it to cover any additional support that you have negotiated.

Work-Life Balance

People place a high value on quality of life and meeting personal needs, as well as monetary recognition for work well done. Quality of life often rests on a delicate balance of work, growth, training and development, personal and family time, and community involvement. The emphasis will vary from one individual to another and over time, but all are important to a rewarding and satisfying lifestyle.

Flexible work arrangements, supplemental vacation time, and extension of benefits to family members are just some of the possibilities for negotiation. Know the company's policies and standard benefits package ahead of time. Read the benefits handbook. If your interests are not adequately addressed, ask topical questions such as the following:

- What is the company policy surrounding quality-of-life issues?

- Can you negotiate extra paid time off—vacation or personal time?

- How is service credit, often the basis for paid time off and other benefits, calculated?

- Are additional vacation days granted for superior individual or organizational performance?

- Does the company shut down, and when?

- Is there a probationary period for certain benefits for newly hired employees?

Be aware that some benefits may have a tax impact. Ascertain what tax obligations, if any, unusual or unfamiliar benefits may carry; or check with an accountant.

If a flexible schedule is a high priority, develop a written proposal after initial interviews. After you start the job, review the arrangement with your management often. In negotiating for an alternative work arrangement or other benefit, make the business case that the accommodation will enhance your productivity. Emphasize your strong commitment and unique individual value to the organization. Anticipate and prepare in advance to address any problems your work schedule might cause with co-workers or customers. Sometimes a trial period is established, so that both management and the employee can test the waters.

Business Expense Reimbursement

The usual manner of paying for employee-incurred business expenses is through a combination of advance cash funds and reimbursement of expenses based on credit card charges or cash receipts. Alternative practice also includes per-diem (daily) allowance payments instead of reimbursement of actual and billed expenses.

If the job will require travel or encompass business entertainment, find out the company's expectations and reimbursement norms during your discussions with the employer. Explore whether a corporate credit card, exclusively for business travel and entertainment, would be practical, and whether a telephone credit card will be supplied for business travel.

Executive and Supplemental Benefits

Most executive employment packages are documented carefully, often as part of an employment contract. These contracts may or may not be structured as automatically renewable.

It is also important to document the settlement of executive and supplemental benefits in the event of separation, whether voluntary or involuntary. In takeover situations, agreement provisions may trigger "golden parachutes," which are enhanced severance arrangements and may provide for accelerated vesting or payout of deferred incentive compensation.

Long-term incentives may be prorated or paid out early, unreduced. The phrase "golden handcuffs" sometimes refers to long-term incentives that pay out only if the individual is actively employed by the organization for a given period of time.

Key Points: Chapter 4

- Total compensation includes salary and variable pay opportunity, benefits, and perquisites.

- A number of variables—including employee knowledge, skill, and experience; the total compensation opportunity; and future compensation prospects—may impact base salary.

- Company-offered benefits most often include health-care plans, income protection, and retirement and termination payments.

- Income-protection plans include sick leave, short-term disability, long-term disability, long-term health care, and life insurance.

- Additional company-offered benefits may include relocation assistance, work and family programs, business travel and entertainment reimbursement, and executive benefits.

Chapter 5

Set Your Negotiation Plan and Strategy

Knowing yourself—who you are professionally, what you have to offer, and what and where you want to be—is your touchstone throughout the negotiation process. Establish your negotiation objectives with an eye to reality, keeping in mind your short- and long-term goals and desired outcomes. Ask yourself, "What are my interests?" "What do I want to achieve?" "What are the logical steps?" "What can I influence?"

Then prioritize "What is critical?" "What do I value?" and "What will meet my needs?" Identify opportunities for compromise: "What can I give up to get what I want?" Know what is of low cost to you but of high benefit to the employer (and vice versa), and know your best alternative—the better and more well thought-out your options, the greater your confidence level. As you learned in chapter 3, having more than one option is a significant source of power in any negotiation.

In this chapter you will learn the steps involved in planning your negotiation beforehand, as well as how to choose and use a negotiation strategy throughout the process.

Planning the Negotiation

Planning means developing a detailed program of action. You are frequently involved in making plans and decisions in your personal life. Your working life, too, can be positively affected by advance planning. Planning for negotiation about the terms and conditions of work increases the likelihood of an enduring and mutually satisfactory work relationship.

Determine the Issues and Your Position

Map the advantages and disadvantages of your proposals. Work on defining the issues. Identify and analyze issues that the employer might have with your proposals and develop ideas to defuse them.

Document your position; support it by referencing common practice, precedents, or generally accepted standards. Prepare to counter employer objections such as, "That's never been done before," or "We don't do that here," by researching and presenting solid supporting information on current trends.

Questions to ask yourself about each issue include the following:

- What is the issue?
- What is my position?
- Why is this my position? What is my rationale, my supporting resource, or my expertise?
- How will the employer view the issue?
  - Anticipate objections.
  - Formulate contingent "if-then" counters.
- What are the significant differences between my position and the employer's, and how will I frame and convey my viewpoint?

Know the Difference Between Wants and Needs

Needs are basic essentials for physical and psychological survival, such as food, shelter, and social interaction. Wants are wishes, usually defined as what we would like to have but can do without. Make sure you need or really want what you are negotiating for. Visualize yourself in your new position. Then do your homework and justify your proposals. By carefully planning the negotiation, you will have the quiet confidence you'll need to project in order to negotiate successfully.

> **Note:** *Remember, job matching means identifying what the employer needs, wants, and values and identifying your corresponding personal and professional assets and qualifications. During the interview process, the employer evaluates a candidate's strengths as they relate to the needs of the business. This helps in predicting employee performance. In turn, you can link the negotiations to the job and to the added value you are bringing to the organization.*

Make a Rough Agenda for the Negotiation

Draft an agenda of topics you want to discuss, but don't make it too rigid in case you have made erroneous assumptions. Unanticipated questions or responses will lead to frustration if you have an uncompromising and over-rehearsed agenda. See the following worksheet for help with drafting your negotiation agenda.

Use this worksheet to map out the issues to be negotiated and to prepare for the response you anticipate the employer will have to your negotiating position. Refer to the sample entry for help.

 NEGOTIATION AGENDA WORKSHEET

Issue: Relocation

Your Position: I am very interested in the job, and I think I would do well with this company. However, I need relocation support to make it possible to move within reasonable commuting distance of the office.

Rationale: I just bought a new home. I have a number of one-time, first year homeowner expenses to recoup, and selling the house myself would take a lot of work and a long time.

Employer Position: I would like to fill the job immediately and have the new employee start work as soon as possible to minimize business disruption. This candidate is highly qualified and would be an asset to the company. However, hiring-policy exceptions are frowned upon here.

Employer Rationale: We are a highly structured organization and I need to adhere to our established relocation program, which provides minimal relocation assistance for a move of less than 60 miles.

Your Response: According to my research, most employers in the area offer relocation assistance to seasoned recruits. The time required to sell the house myself doesn't make sense given the urgency to bring me on board. Would you consider a signing bonus that would help me manage the cost of selling the house? I then would be free to undertake the search for a new home right away.

Issue: _____

_____

Your Position: _____

_____

_____

(continued)

(continued)

Rationale: _____

_____

_____

Employer Position: _____

_____

_____

Employer Rationale: _____

_____

_____

Your Response: _____

_____

_____

Issue: _____

Your Position: _____

_____

_____

Rationale: _____

_____

_____

Employer Position: _____

_____

_____

Employer Rationale: _____

_____

_____

Your Response: _____

_____

Forming Your Strategy

Strategy is the art of maximizing your plan's effectiveness by selectively focusing all available resources toward achieving your goal. Here are some tips for formulating your negotiation strategy.

Prepare Mentally

The strategy you develop for a negotiation should reflect your goals and leverage your strengths, while downplaying any weaknesses. Take control of the process by creating a mental picture of your negotiation strategy, developing supporting points, and brushing up on negotiation skills (see chapter 6). By doing these things, you will significantly increase the probability of a successful outcome.

> **Tip:** *Some people find that they can reach the optimal mindset by repeating an affirmation to themselves, such as, "I am well prepared for negotiation; I handle negotiations confidently and successfully."*

Build your confidence by confirming your situational power sources and impact areas, which you identified in chapter 3. Power sources include economics, supply-and-demand considerations, time constraints, precedents and practices, your short- and long-term goals, and choice—the other viable options you have.

Manage the Process

To the extent possible, establish a safe environment in which both parties feel comfortable. Soft negotiations are governed by a manner of working together and clearly differentiating between the people (the relationship) and the problem (the issues) involved. People have different points of view and different beliefs about what is really important.

Use a Win-Win Approach

Approach the employer amicably, as an active partner, rather than defensively. Be prepared to initiate a discussion, setting the stage for the negotiation by talking about the negotiation process and customary procedure. Agree on the criteria for evaluating the quality of the discussion.

Look at the negotiation as an opportunity to exchange ideas and build the best work arrangement for both you and the employer. This is a chance to present yourself in a cooperative and collaborative light. Use your interpersonal and communication skills to create rapport. Ground your negotiation by aligning your interests with those of the employer. Frequently reaffirm your interest in working for the company and in the position. Emphasize your ability to contribute to the success of the business.

Identify and Address the Issues

Begin the negotiation by complimenting the positive aspects of the job offer on the table. Bring up your desired changes to the offer in the context of the whole offer, confirming the points on which you both agree. Sometimes it is wise to start negotiating with a smaller request, to test the waters, and then tackle more difficult issues. But don't waste negotiating power on trivial points.

Negotiation often involves some degree of compromise. By planning, you've determined what you must have—and what you are willing to exchange. You know what your interests are, and you have differentiated between what you need and what you want. Your solution, however, may not be the only solution. Rather than take an unyielding position, suggest acceptable alternatives to your requests.

Think from the organization's perspective, and be aware of the disadvantages of high turnover to the employer. Turnover costs can include a former employee's severance payments and benefits continuation, unemployment taxes, and new-hire recruiting and training expenses, as well as the loss of productivity. It is usually in the employer's interest to do whatever is feasible to attract and retain a diverse, highly skilled workforce.

Present your case and cast your proposals in the light of common sense and business costs and benefits. Be prepared with a ready rationale to relate your position to employer interests, and have reasonable solutions to anticipated objections. Acknowledge objections and move on; if an issue is critical, return to the subject in question later in the discussion. Be sure to have your thoughts organized. In the planning phase, think in terms of easy-to-remember "threes"—assemble three points to support each of your positions.

Manage Expectations

You decided your limits in the planning stage, before beginning the actual negotiations. Position yourself to make counter-offers to the employer's offer. Respond by first reaffirming your interest and qualifications, and then make your suggestion. Stay flexible and always keep the negotiations open. Be comfortable with silence and avoid overstating your case.

Stay on Track

Remain focused on the value that hiring you will bring to the company. Appeals to the common good, the company's image, or others' opinions are not issue-oriented. Have available and refer to independent practices and pay and benefits standards (see chapter 7 of this book).

If you find yourself in the position of having to make a concession on an issue, evaluate the concession objectively. Ask yourself "How much will this concession cost? What can I expect in return?" Remember that concessions should be earned, not volunteered. Know when to stand your ground reasonably and when to let go of an issue.

The axiom that "you have to give in order to get" holds true. As part of your strategy, plan what material you can give ahead of time and give only what you can afford. For example, you might be willing to give up something you want—such as extended vacation time—in exchange for the ongoing flexibility you really need during the work week to accommodate child-care demands.

Be Realistic

The dynamics of negotiations are often subtle. Watch for negative signals from the other party. Don't allow the negotiation to be jeopardized or to collapse unnecessarily. Presenting a long list of relatively small items risks creating the impression that you might be difficult to work with. A candidate who is inordinately concerned about the company's policies on vacation time, scheduled holidays, and overtime, for example, might be perceived as lacking a commitment to the goals of the business. Use good judgment in presenting and pursuing your personal agenda.

Key Points: Chapter 5

- Advance planning paves the way for successful negotiation.
- Strategy is about what methods you will use to move successfully through the negotiation process.
- During negotiation, continually stress mutual benefit, cost consciousness, and added value.

Chapter 6

Negotiating Techniques and Tips

Now that all of your planning and preparation are done, you're ready to face the employer and begin negotiations. Skilled communication is the key element in a successful negotiation. This chapter will help you listen well and communicate your needs effectively.

Effective Negotiation Communication

Interpersonal communication is an ongoing interactive process through which we create meaning, send and receive messages and feedback, and confirm or adjust our understanding of the messages being conveyed.

In putting it all together, how we communicate—framing, advocating, illustrating, and inquiring—creates a lasting impression on others. Solid, persuasive communications skills are required to get the message across effectively. By establishing rapport and a win-win climate of openness up front, you set the tone for successful negotiations.

Approaching the Negotiation

Assess the audience—the person(s) you will be negotiating with—and adopt an appropriate communication style. Organize a main theme and identify key points. Concentrate on how your uniqueness will add value to the business, while contributing to controlling costs. Demonstrate your potential effect on new initiatives and/or productivity. Make the decision ahead of time whether to begin with a minor issue that will be easy to resolve or to present an issue of major importance to you. Always think and speak about the long-term effects of your joining the company.

The Exploration Stage

Initiate the discussion with a positive statement and then wait for feedback. Frame the negotiation with a general statement of your mutual goals. In the exploration period, confirm or adjust your perceptions of the employer's needs. Demonstrate that you understand the other party's position, perhaps by using comparison or analogy.

Build trust. Gain agreement on aligned issues. Stress your commitment and credibility, as well as your expertise, competence, and ability to get things done. Maintain an air of reasonability. In win-win negotiations, the goal is to work together to look for a mutually agreeable outcome. Keep the focus on what both parties want.

The Relationship

Valuing the relationship you have established with the employer is paramount. Remember that you will be working with the person with whom you are negotiating. Pushing too hard, taking a hard line or an adversarial posture, or letting the discussion deteriorate into a contest are counterproductive in the long run.

When an issue surfaces, avoid attempts to personalize it. Appreciate that you and the employer have different needs to be met, rather than thinking in win-lose terms. Use tact and diplomacy. Make it your personal creed when engaged in negotiation to help the other party "save face."

Language

Persuasion is the ability to change or influence a belief. Persuade rather than coerce the other party. Use inclusive phrases and "if" statements. Establish a common ground for agreement; for example, "If we accept that it will be necessary for me to work every other Saturday, would you agree that some additional vacation time might be arranged?" Practice phrasing a compromise opening, such as, "What if" or "How about," or "Would you feel." Frequently restate (or "echo") what the other person says. Create, and be comfortable with, conversational and reflective silence. Ask, but don't assume!

Always try to negotiate face to face. This is especially valuable in the initial negotiations, when you are establishing trust. Body language is important. Convey goodwill and attentiveness with your facial expressions and a relaxed, open posture. Dress and look the part of your new job.

Use "what," not "why," to ask questions. Conditional language that softens the message when appropriate, such as the following phrases, greatly facilitates negotiations. Never react with a flat "no"; rather, pause, consider thoughtfully, then respond:

"That is not going to work."

Continue reasonably, with an appropriate phrase; for example, use language such as the following:

- "Are you willing to…?"
- "What would you consider?"
- "What are the alternatives?"
- "I understand your concerns."
- "I am able/I can…"
- "Do you agree that…?"
- "There are some things I would like to discuss."
- "I would like to consider/Have you considered…?"
- "Have you thought about…?"
- "Oh, by the way…"
- "What is reasonable?"
- "Generally…"
- "What is the opportunity for…?"
- "What if/in lieu of…?"
- "What is the approval process?"
- "I would like your thoughts on…"
- "These are my problems."
- "Can we talk about…?"
- "Can we explore the possibility of…?"
- "Is there anything you might be able to do about…?"
- "The trend today seems to be/One of the things that is quite common in the industry is…"
- "There are a few things I am having a problem with…"
- "Is there anything/anything else the company can do?"
- "At what level do _____ kick in?" (bonuses/benefits/perks)

Conflict

Conflict can be constructive and positive. Some level of discord is inevitable; disagreement and conflict are a natural part of the negotiation process. The give-and-take of different points of view serves a purpose, helping determine what is important to each party. Working through conflict clarifies thinking and the needs, not just the wants or general interests, of the other party.

Remain objective and focused on your priorities. In most negotiations, patterns can be distinguished relative to the terms of "give and get," such as both giving, giving if getting, and so forth. Remember, conflict is only disagreement, and it's a necessary part of the negotiation process. Refusal to meet your requirements is not rejection of you as an individual or as a future employee.

Beware of making absolute statements in your negotiations. Describe the benefits of your proposals to the employer. In a stalemate, neither side is willing to move and the negotiation fails. Approach a difficult issue by asking yourself, "How can I resolve this?" "How could the employer resolve this?" What adjustments or conditions would facilitate resolution, and what could be expected in return?

Continue to identify and assess options and possible approaches to settling issues throughout the negotiation process. Remember that nothing is free. A good agreement requires both participants to give and receive concessions; what the negotiation determines is only how much, and when.

Let's Stay in Touch

When you meet resistance, be persistent, but know when to let go. If negotiations cannot be concluded on the spot, ask the following questions:

- "Are there any reservations, or reasons that my proposals wouldn't be considered?"
- "What are our next steps and what is the timing?"

When you get stuck, take a break, make a small concession, or offer to meet halfway. Suggest integrative solutions, which are more likely to move the negotiation forward. Never be adversarial, but rather explore possibilities and continue to extend the same flexibility and understanding you are hoping to receive.

Closing

Know when to conclude. And when you do conclude, hold your ground pleasantly. Be patient. Don't press too quickly for closure. Allow some quiet moments to consider what is on the table.

Once a satisfactory agreement is arrived at, summarize it verbally. Then send a follow-up letter to verify the verbal agreement. Introduce your follow-up letter by mentioning your pleasure with the process and the relationship. Then write something like "Following is a summary of my understanding of our agreement" or "This is my understanding of what we agreed to." Conclude with a positive statement about the agreement and an expression of your appreciation.

If, after careful consideration, you determine that you and the employer have been unable to reach a mutually satisfactory understanding, be sure to call to let him or her know of your decision. Then send a letter of declination, expressing your appreciation for the offer and keeping the door open for future opportunities to work together.

In some instances, you might be considering more than one offer simultaneously. In communicating with competing employers, it's usually best to be up-front about the situation, but be sure to avoid any appearance of playing one offer against the other. Once you have made a decision, notify the employer of choice, and then the competing employer.

When declining, stress the appeal of the offers and companies and point out that for many reasons, you chose the offer most suited to you personally at this point in time. Follow up with a sincere thank-you letter, conveying your appreciation of the offer and the time spent with you, and suggesting you keep in touch with one another. In this era of business networking and constant change, you might be working together in the future, one way or another!

The Importance of Active Listening Skills

One of the most critical interpersonal communications skills is the ability to listen well. With active listening, the listener reflects back (repeats) what he has heard to acknowledge understanding and provide the opportunity for further clarification. Active listening emphasizes sensitivity to the other party's reactions and feelings and the ability to see things from their point of view.

Listening skills encompass frequent restatement of positions through asking clarifying questions, emphasizing points of agreement, and adopting a "team" or "we could" attitude. As the negotiation proceeds, active listening becomes highly contributory to a successful outcome. Communication must be responsive to the situation and to the sometimes unpredictable or unintentional messages that the other party is sending.

Don't assume that you understand what the employer is saying—or vice versa. Use active listening to reflect your initial understanding of the information that has been conveyed. Checking back by asking questions allows you to assess progress and avoid possible derailment along the route to a successful agreement.

As the negotiation progresses, ask yourself questions such as these:

- How is the other party expressing issues and concerns?

- Are there hidden needs not yet acknowledged that must be brought to the surface?

- Are incompatibilities being defined and addressed?

Negotiation Techniques

Many techniques can influence the outcome of negotiations. Some involve the content; for example, packaging—splitting or combining (bundling) issues for discussion in an effort to present the matter in the most favorable light, or tabling a difficult issue and revisiting it later. Others focus on negotiating style; for example, consciously separating the individuals (personalities) from the issues and attending to both.

The following table contains some positive and negative negotiating techniques. Review these techniques so that you can use a particular positive approach when it would be advantageous (and avoid unscrupulous ones). It's also helpful to be able to recognize when someone else is using a defined negotiation technique.

MANIPULATIVE	COULD BE MANIPULATIVE OR LEGITIMATE APPROACH	UP-FRONT COMMUNICATION
Making deceptive or testing statements; lessens trust and may imply power-linked intimidation	Evaluating in context	Encouraging trust and win-win agreement
Controlling the agenda or having a hidden agenda	Proposing an agenda	Beginning with a review of aligned interests
Lowballing and "Mother Hubbard" (the cupboard is bare)	Offering observations about current trends and conditions	Making a statement of fair dealing
Feinting—bluffing or placing exaggerated importance on a lesser point	Asking for something that incorporates an objective	Redefining the issue; reframing
Imposing deadlines and time pressures	Withdrawing or (perceived) retreat; waiting the other side out	Maintaining reflective silence; deferring decision (breaking to re-evaluate)
"Columbo"— "One more thing"— add-ons	Presenting the surprise proposal	Using conditional language
Forcing a choice between two bad alternatives— Russian Front	Splitting the difference	Tactfully challenging a statement

(continued)

(continued)

MANIPULATIVE	COULD BE MANIPULATIVE OR LEGITIMATE APPROACH	UP-FRONT COMMUNICATION
Claiming limited authority to make the decision—good guy/ bad guy (the Denver System)	Obtaining concessions a little at a time— "salami"	Pinpointing the business need
Referencing as standard practice and assume it's a done deal before accepting or declining— Fait Accompli	Bundling or unbundling	Requesting time to consider the terms of the renegotiated offer

Use the following checklist to make sure you are ready to communicate effectively in the negotiation.

NEGOTIATION COMMUNICATIONS CHECKLIST

Preparation

❏ Research the company.

❏ Plan your presentation relative to the job. Prepare examples, positive responses, and thoughtful alternatives.

Rehearsal

❏ Practice.

❏ Speak out loud.

❏ Use a reasonable tone of voice.

Appearance

❏ Be appropriately attired and well groomed.

❏ Maintain a professional demeanor.

Communication

❏ Speak in a well-modulated tone.

❏ Make eye contact.

❏ Use effective body language.

❏ Listen actively.

❏ Relax. Smile!

Package

❏ Assemble relevant reference materials.

❏ Bring samples of your work products, if relevant.

Key Points: Chapter 6

- Communications skills are a significant advantage in negotiation.

- Positive phrasing of points and proposals is important.

- Listening actively will give you clues and additional cues to which you can consciously tailor your responses.

- Active listening enhances negotiation communications significantly and reduces the likelihood of misunderstandings.

- Be certain to use ethical negotiation tactics, and be on the lookout for an employer who uses unscrupulous ones.

Chapter 7

Directory of National Salary Averages

The following data on salary averages was compiled by the U.S. Department of Labor's Bureau of Labor Statistics. The 268 jobs listed here are based on 2005 Occupational Outlook data from the Bureau of Labor Statistics (the latest data available at the time of publication). These jobs represent nearly 80 percent of the U.S. workforce.

For each job, you will find a listing of the average person's earnings in the job, what beginning workers usually earn, and what the workers at the 25th and 75th percentiles earn.

Where available, we have listed the average earnings in the job in up to 10 major metropolitan areas. For some jobs, there is not a significant number of workers in each metro area. In those cases, we have omitted one or more of the cities.

We also provide the average earnings for the job in several of the top industries that employ people in that job. This is an interesting illustration of how the industry in which you work can affect your earnings.

Tip: *The Bureau of Labor Statistics updates its salary figures every year.* Check the Occupational Outlook Handbook *online at www.bls.gov/oco for updated information.*

And finally, heed our earlier advice to compare job descriptions as well as job titles. You can find descriptions for all these jobs online at www.bls.gov/oco/. Be sure to use the salary data for the job that most closely matches what you do.

ACCOUNTANTS AND AUDITORS

- Average Earnings: $52,210
- Beginning Earnings: $33,170
- 25th Percentile: $40,900
- 75th Percentile: $68,430

Average Earnings in Major Metropolitan Areas

Metropolitan Area	Average Annual Earnings
Atlanta, GA	$51,170
Chicago, IL	$55,280
Dallas-Fort Worth, TX	$53,940
Denver, CO	$53,810
Los Angeles, CA	$54,170
Minneapolis-St. Paul, MN	$52,850
New York, NY	$65,050
Phoenix, AZ	$48,880
San Francisco, CA	$60,880
Seattle, WA	$55,770

Average Earnings in Most Important Industries

Industry	Average Annual Earnings
Professional, Scientific, and Technical Services	$54,340
Management of Companies and Enterprises	$53,370
Administrative and Support Services	$49,860
Credit Intermediation and Related Activities	$49,860
Federal, State, and Local Government	$48,500

ACTORS, PRODUCERS, AND DIRECTORS

- Average Earnings: $53,860
- Beginning Earnings: $26,870
- 25th Percentile: $36,650
- 75th Percentile: $84,610

Average Earnings in Major Metropolitan Areas

Metropolitan Area	Average Annual Earnings
Atlanta, GA	$54,360
Chicago, IL	$62,920
Dallas-Fort Worth, TX	$52,690
Denver, CO	$52,550
Los Angeles, CA	$72,210
Minneapolis-St. Paul, MN	$48,100
New York, NY	$81,710
Phoenix, AZ	$45,040
San Francisco, CA	$79,980
Seattle, WA	$46,040

Average Earnings in Most Important Industries

Industry	Average Annual Earnings
Motion Picture and Sound Recording Industries	$70,820
Professional, Scientific, and Technical Services	$69,870
Broadcasting (Except Internet)	$48,650
Educational Services	$44,150
Performing Arts, Spectator Sports, and Related Industries	$42,640

Note: Averages apply only to Producers and Directors.

ACTUARIES

- Average Earnings: $81,640
- Beginning Earnings: $45,660
- 25th Percentile: $57,740
- 75th Percentile: $112,360

Average Earnings in Major Metropolitan Areas

Metropolitan Area	Average Annual Earnings
Atlanta, GA	$76,040
Chicago, IL	$88,310
Dallas-Fort Worth, TX	$96,630
Los Angeles, CA	$87,700
New York, NY	$98,870
San Francisco, CA	$85,680

Average Earnings in Most Important Industries

Industry	Average Annual Earnings
Professional, Scientific, and Technical Services	$94,080
Funds, Trusts, and Other Financial Vehicles	$86,290
Insurance Carriers and Related Activities	$80,900
Federal, State, and Local Government	$73,040
Management of Companies and Enterprises	$70,380

ADMINISTRATIVE SERVICES MANAGERS

- Average Earnings: $64,020
- Beginning Earnings: $32,770
- 25th Percentile: $45,460
- 75th Percentile: $86,730

Average Earnings in Major Metropolitan Areas

Metropolitan Area	Average Annual Earnings
Atlanta, GA	$63,240
Chicago, IL	$54,680
Dallas-Fort Worth, TX	$73,740
Denver, CO	$67,700
Los Angeles, CA	$74,210
Minneapolis-St. Paul, MN	$74,300
New York, NY	$85,440
Phoenix, AZ	$47,470
San Francisco, CA	$81,410
Seattle, WA	$79,300

Average Earnings in Most Important Industries

Industry	Average Annual Earnings
Professional, Scientific, and Technical Services	$70,110
Hospitals	$66,720
Federal, State, and Local Government	$63,540
Educational Services	$63,170
Administrative and Support Services	$55,200

ADVERTISING SALES AGENTS

- Average Earnings: $41,770
- Beginning Earnings: $21,080
- 25th Percentile: $28,840
- 75th Percentile: $61,920

Average Earnings in Major Metropolitan Areas

Metropolitan Area	Average Annual Earnings
Atlanta, GA	$42,870
Chicago, IL	$39,080
Dallas-Fort Worth, TX	$37,550
Denver, CO	$43,060
Los Angeles, CA	$46,600
Minneapolis-St. Paul, MN	$54,610
New York, NY	$52,570
San Francisco, CA	$54,880
Seattle, WA	$50,160

Average Earnings in Most Important Industries

Industry	Average Annual Earnings
Motion Picture and Sound Recording Industries	$46,380
Professional, Scientific, and Technical Services	$45,820
Telecommunications	$45,350
Broadcasting (Except Internet)	$41,580
Publishing Industries (Except Internet)	$36,490

ADVERTISING, MARKETING, PROMOTIONS, PUBLIC RELATIONS, AND SALES MANAGERS

- Average Earnings: $86,845
- Beginning Earnings: $43,632
- 25th Percentile: $59,832
- 75th Percentile: $125,004

Average Earnings in Major Metropolitan Areas

Metropolitan Area	Average Annual Earnings
Atlanta, GA	$89,423
Chicago, IL	$86,365
Dallas-Fort Worth, TX	$91,669
Denver, CO	$91,496
Los Angeles, CA	$96,562
Minneapolis-St. Paul, MN	$103,884
New York, NY	$122,338
Phoenix, AZ	$71,966
San Francisco, CA	$108,206
Seattle, WA	$108,407

Average Earnings in Most Important Industries

Industry	Average Annual Earnings
Professional, Scientific, and Technical Services	$103,217
Management of Companies and Enterprises	$95,160
Merchant Wholesalers, Durable Goods	$93,365
Merchant Wholesalers, Nondurable Goods	$88,439
Administrative and Support Services	$70,917

AGRICULTURAL AND FOOD SCIENTISTS

- Average Earnings: $51,750
- Beginning Earnings: $30,731
- 25th Percentile: $38,256
- 75th Percentile: $69,411

Average Earnings in Major Metropolitan Areas

Metropolitan Area	Average Annual Earnings
Atlanta, GA	$45,010
Chicago, IL	$55,420
Dallas-Fort Worth, TX	$81,080
Denver, CO	$88,830
Los Angeles, CA	$58,810
Minneapolis-St. Paul, MN	$66,456
New York, NY	$60,517
San Francisco, CA	$60,140
Seattle, WA	$70,831

Average Earnings in Most Important Industries

Industry	Average Annual Earnings
Merchant Wholesalers, Nondurable Goods	$62,688
Federal, State, and Local Government	$61,099
Professional, Scientific, and Technical Services	$53,365
Food Manufacturing	$44,667
Educational Services	$41,998

AGRICULTURAL WORKERS

- Average Earnings: $17,613
- Beginning Earnings: $13,792
- 25th Percentile: $15,440
- 75th Percentile: $20,448

Average Earnings in Major Metropolitan Areas

Metropolitan Area	Average Annual Earnings
Atlanta, GA	$21,646
Chicago, IL	$20,613
Dallas-Fort Worth, TX	$16,393
Denver, CO	$21,254
Los Angeles, CA	$17,708
Minneapolis-St. Paul, MN	$25,129
New York, NY	$21,397
Phoenix, AZ	$13,655
San Francisco, CA	$21,053
Seattle, WA	$20,427

Average Earnings in Most Important Industries

Industry	Average Annual Earnings
Federal, State, and Local Government	$31,254
Food Manufacturing	$19,230
Merchant Wholesalers, Nondurable Goods	$17,720
Support Activities for Agriculture and Forestry	$16,530
Administrative and Support Services	$16,353

AIR TRAFFIC CONTROLLERS

- Average Earnings: $107,590
- Beginning Earnings: $60,340
- 25th Percentile: $81,090
- 75th Percentile: $130,640

Average Earnings in Major Metropolitan Areas

Metropolitan Area	Average Annual Earnings
Atlanta, GA	$128,780
Chicago, IL	$126,990
Dallas-Fort Worth, TX	$97,130
Denver, CO	$117,010
Los Angeles, CA	$117,410
Minneapolis-St. Paul, MN	$122,010
New York, NY	$129,100
Phoenix, AZ	$98,180
San Francisco, CA	$127,400

Average Earnings in Most Important Industries

Industry	Average Annual Earnings
Federal, State, and Local Government	$111,950

AIRCRAFT AND AVIONICS EQUIPMENT MECHANICS AND SERVICE TECHNICIANS

- Average Earnings: $47,199
- Beginning Earnings: $31,065
- 25th Percentile: $38,474
- 75th Percentile: $57,784

Average Earnings in Major Metropolitan Areas

Metropolitan Area	Average Annual Earnings
Atlanta, GA	$53,370
Chicago, IL	$52,250
Denver, CO	$53,652
Los Angeles, CA	$54,008
Minneapolis-St. Paul, MN	$47,650
New York, NY	$52,370
Phoenix, AZ	$47,603
Seattle, WA	$59,534

Average Earnings in Most Important Industries

Industry	Average Annual Earnings
Couriers and Messengers	$73,330
Air Transportation	$56,040
Federal, State, and Local Government	$47,075
Transportation Equipment Manufacturing	$44,624
Support Activities for Transportation	$39,698

AIRCRAFT PILOTS AND FLIGHT ENGINEERS

- Average Earnings: $117,918
- Beginning Earnings: $45,855
- 25th Percentile: $72,024
- 75th Percentile: $20,281

Average Earnings in Major Metropolitan Areas

Metropolitan Area	Average Annual Earnings
Atlanta, GA	$65,560
Chicago, IL	$139,954
Dallas-Fort Worth, TX	$46,940
Denver, CO	$111,770
Los Angeles, CA	$111,543
Minneapolis-St. Paul, MN	$78,040
New York, NY	$87,080
Phoenix, AZ	$35,040
Seattle, WA	$45,830

Average Earnings in Most Important Industries

Industry	Average Annual Earnings
Air Transportation	$137,228

Note: 75th percentile figure applies only to Commercial Pilots.

ANIMAL CARE AND SERVICE WORKERS

- Average Earnings: $18,261
- Beginning Earnings: $13,529
- 25th Percentile: $15,496
- 75th Percentile: $23,436

Average Earnings in Major Metropolitan Areas

Metropolitan Area	Average Annual Earnings
Atlanta, GA	$17,394
Chicago, IL	$18,877
Dallas-Fort Worth, TX	$16,830
Denver, CO	$20,374
Los Angeles, CA	$18,735
Minneapolis-St. Paul, MN	$18,400
New York, NY	$20,913
Phoenix, AZ	$16,820
San Francisco, CA	$25,103
Seattle, WA	$19,080

Average Earnings in Most Important Industries

Industry	Average Annual Earnings
Performing Arts, Spectator Sports, and Related Industries	$20,490
Personal and Laundry Services	$19,133
Religious, Grantmaking, Civic, Professional, and Similar Organizations	$17,303
Professional, Scientific, and Technical Services	$16,740
Miscellaneous Store Retailers	$16,726

ANNOUNCERS

- Average Earnings: $23,983
- Beginning Earnings: $13,338
- 25th Percentile: $16,610
- 75th Percentile: $37,967

Average Earnings in Major Metropolitan Areas

Metropolitan Area	Average Annual Earnings
Atlanta, GA	$27,963
Chicago, IL	$36,057
Dallas-Fort Worth, TX	$23,664
Denver, CO	$29,924
Los Angeles, CA	$30,487
Minneapolis-St. Paul, MN	$28,376
New York, NY	$52,596
Phoenix, AZ	$32,960
San Francisco, CA	$37,000
Seattle, WA	$26,050

Average Earnings in Most Important Industries

Industry	Average Annual Earnings
Performing Arts, Spectator Sports, and Related Industries	$28,580
Educational Services	$26,512
Broadcasting (Except Internet)	$23,681
Food Services and Drinking Places	$19,680
Amusement, Gambling, and Recreation Industries	$17,571

APPRAISERS AND ASSESSORS OF REAL ESTATE

- Average Earnings: $43,440
- Beginning Earnings: $23,020
- 25th Percentile: $30,990
- 75th Percentile: $62,100

Average Earnings in Major Metropolitan Areas

Metropolitan Area	Average Annual Earnings
Atlanta, GA	$39,420
Chicago, IL	$54,330
Dallas-Fort Worth, TX	$69,650
Denver, CO	$60,850
Minneapolis-St. Paul, MN	$53,980
New York, NY	$58,940
Phoenix, AZ	$43,060
San Francisco, CA	$74,500

Average Earnings in Most Important Industries

Industry	Average Annual Earnings
Management of Companies and Enterprises	$65,450
Credit Intermediation and Related Activities	$58,440
Real Estate	$46,710
Federal, State, and Local Government	$40,040
Professional, Scientific, and Technical Services	$37,430

ARCHITECTS, EXCEPT LANDSCAPE AND NAVAL

- Average Earnings: $62,850
- Beginning Earnings: $39,130
- 25th Percentile: $48,670
- 75th Percentile: $81,680

Average Earnings in Major Metropolitan Areas

Metropolitan Area	Average Annual Earnings
Atlanta, GA	$69,060
Chicago, IL	$65,480
Dallas-Fort Worth, TX	$66,880
Denver, CO	$60,260
Los Angeles, CA	$65,360
Minneapolis-St. Paul, MN	$61,700
New York, NY	$66,480
Phoenix, AZ	$64,040
San Francisco, CA	$73,930
Seattle, WA	$64,660

Average Earnings in Most Important Industries

Industry	Average Annual Earnings
Professional, Scientific, and Technical Services	$62,150

ARCHIVISTS, CURATORS, AND MUSEUM TECHNICIANS

- Average Earnings: $39,013
- Beginning Earnings: $22,480
- 25th Percentile: $29,290
- 75th Percentile: $51,784

Average Earnings in Major Metropolitan Areas

Metropolitan Area	Average Annual Earnings
Atlanta, GA	$35,262
Chicago, IL	$39,404
Dallas-Fort Worth, TX	$31,450
Denver, CO	$44,304
Los Angeles, CA	$47,386
Minneapolis-St. Paul, MN	$44,660
New York, NY	$43,924
Phoenix, AZ	$36,200
San Francisco, CA	$60,279
Seattle, WA	$38,672

Average Earnings in Most Important Industries

Industry	Average Annual Earnings
Educational Services	$41,103
Federal, State, and Local Government	$40,728
Museums, Historical Sites, and Similar Institutions	$37,243
Motion Picture and Sound Recording Industries	$36,470
Religious, Grantmaking, Civic, Professional, and Similar Organizations	$31,602

ARTISTS AND RELATED WORKERS

- Average Earnings: $53,054
- Beginning Earnings: $30,096
- 25th Percentile: $39,664
- 75th Percentile: $73,778

Average Earnings in Major Metropolitan Areas

Metropolitan Area	Average Annual Earnings
Atlanta, GA	$54,052
Chicago, IL	$57,857
Dallas-Fort Worth, TX	$51,980
Denver, CO	$52,756
Los Angeles, CA	$71,123
Minneapolis-St. Paul, MN	$54,966
New York, NY	$74,196
Phoenix, AZ	$43,621
San Francisco, CA	$80,453
Seattle, WA	$63,638

Average Earnings in Most Important Industries

Industry	Average Annual Earnings
Motion Picture and Sound Recording Industries	$60,442
Professional, Scientific, and Technical Services	$59,453
Publishing Industries (Except Internet)	$53,489
Performing Arts, Spectator Sports, and Related Industries	$36,025
Nonmetallic Mineral Product Manufacturing	$23,195

ASSEMBLERS AND FABRICATORS

- Average Earnings: $25,408
- Beginning Earnings: $16,470
- 25th Percentile: $19,944
- 75th Percentile: $33,235

Average Earnings in Major Metropolitan Areas

Metropolitan Area	Average Annual Earnings
Atlanta, GA	$28,621
Chicago, IL	$22,288
Dallas-Fort Worth, TX	$22,970
Denver, CO	$23,793
Los Angeles, CA	$20,963
Minneapolis-St. Paul, MN	$28,001
New York, NY	$23,516
Phoenix, AZ	$23,331
San Francisco, CA	$26,763
Seattle, WA	$28,579

Average Earnings in Most Important Industries

Industry	Average Annual Earnings
Transportation Equipment Manufacturing	$33,498
Machinery Manufacturing	$27,741
Fabricated Metal Product Manufacturing	$25,736
Computer and Electronic Product Manufacturing	$24,796
Administrative and Support Services	$19,319

ATHLETES, COACHES, UMPIRES, AND RELATED WORKERS

- Average Earnings: $26,661
- Beginning Earnings: $13,737
- 25th Percentile: $17,657
- 75th Percentile: $42,906

Average Earnings in Major Metropolitan Areas

Metropolitan Area	Average Annual Earnings
Atlanta, GA	$31,700
Chicago, IL	$20,983
Dallas-Fort Worth, TX	$26,190
Denver, CO	$27,067
Los Angeles, CA	$26,368
Minneapolis-St. Paul, MN	$30,409
New York, NY	$35,531
Phoenix, AZ	$22,937
San Francisco, CA	$29,110
Seattle, WA	$29,790

Average Earnings in Most Important Industries

Industry	Average Annual Earnings
Performing Arts, Spectator Sports, and Related Industries	$38,002
Amusement, Gambling, and Recreation Industries	$26,415
Educational Services	$25,939
Federal, State, and Local Government	$24,424
Religious, Grantmaking, Civic, Professional, and Similar Organizations	$21,604

Note: 75th percentile figure applies only to Coaches and Scouts and to Umpires, Referees, and Other Sports Officials.

ATHLETIC TRAINERS

- Average Earnings: $34,260
- Beginning Earnings: $20,240
- 25th Percentile: $26,930
- 75th Percentile: $43,080

Average Earnings in Major Metropolitan Areas

Metropolitan Area	Average Annual Earnings
Denver, CO	$46,470
New York, NY	$38,990
Phoenix, AZ	$38,510
Chicago, IL	$32,350
Los Angeles, CA	$22,120

Average Earnings in Most Important Industries

Industry	Average Annual Earnings
Educational Services	$38,270
Hospitals	$36,390
Ambulatory Health Care Services	$34,610
Amusement, Gambling, and Recreation Industries	$28,120
Federal, State, and Local Government	$25,330

ATMOSPHERIC SCIENTISTS

- Average Earnings: $73,940
- Beginning Earnings: $37,250
- 25th Percentile: $52,410
- 75th Percentile: $89,500

Average Earnings in Major Metropolitan Areas

Metropolitan Area	Average Annual Earnings
Atlanta, GA	$83,000
Chicago, IL	$62,870
Minneapolis-St. Paul, MN	$69,360
New York, NY	$89,130
San Francisco, CA	$82,730

Average Earnings in Most Important Industries

Industry	Average Annual Earnings
Computer and Electronic Product Manufacturing	$95,710
Federal, State, and Local Government	$80,790
Broadcasting (Except Internet)	$67,800
Professional, Scientific, and Technical Services	$63,290
Educational Services	$59,030

AUDIOLOGISTS

- Average Earnings: $53,490
- Beginning Earnings: $35,920
- 25th Percentile: $44,400
- 75th Percentile: $65,710

Average Earnings in Major Metropolitan Areas

Metropolitan Area	Average Annual Earnings
Chicago, IL	$49,900
Dallas-Fort Worth, TX	$56,530
Denver, CO	$57,880
Minneapolis-St. Paul, MN	$56,760
New York, NY	$62,870
Phoenix, AZ	$48,970
Seattle, WA	$63,720

Average Earnings in Most Important Industries

Industry	Average Annual Earnings
Ambulatory Health Care Services	$54,030
Hospitals	$54,880
Health and Personal Care Stores	$51,650
Federal, State, and Local Government	$51,480
Educational Services	$51,220

AUTOMOTIVE BODY AND RELATED REPAIRERS

- Average Earnings: $34,274
- Beginning Earnings: $20,227
- 25th Percentile: $26,233
- 75th Percentile: $45,031

Average Earnings in Major Metropolitan Areas

Metropolitan Area	Average Annual Earnings
Atlanta, GA	$44,270
Chicago, IL	$40,816
Dallas-Fort Worth, TX	$32,851
Denver, CO	$49,350
Los Angeles, CA	$38,850
Minneapolis-St. Paul, MN	$42,945
New York, NY	$35,118
Phoenix, AZ	$34,320
San Francisco, CA	$46,396
Seattle, WA	$41,220

Average Earnings in Most Important Industries

Industry	Average Annual Earnings
Motor Vehicle and Parts Dealers	$35,115
Repair and Maintenance	$33,915

AUTOMOTIVE SERVICE TECHNICIANS AND MECHANICS

- Average Earnings: $33,050
- Beginning Earnings: $18,500
- 25th Percentile: $24,090
- 75th Percentile: $43,580

Average Earnings in Major Metropolitan Areas

Metropolitan Area	Average Annual Earnings
Atlanta, GA	$36,000
Chicago, IL	$34,540
Dallas-Fort Worth, TX	$33,120
Denver, CO	$36,140
Los Angeles, CA	$33,870
Minneapolis-St. Paul, MN	$35,650
New York, NY	$34,700
Phoenix, AZ	$37,220
San Francisco, CA	$46,050
Seattle, WA	$42,330

Average Earnings in Most Important Industries

Industry	Average Annual Earnings
Federal, State, and Local Government	$39,260
Motor Vehicle and Parts Dealers	$36,090
Merchant Wholesalers, Durable Goods	$31,860
Repair and Maintenance	$29,790
Gasoline Stations	$27,950

BARBERS, COSMETOLOGISTS, AND OTHER PERSONAL APPEARANCE WORKERS

- Average Earnings: $20,380
- Beginning Earnings: $13,448
- 25th Percentile: $15,872
- 75th Percentile: $27,074

Average Earnings in Major Metropolitan Areas

Metropolitan Area	Average Annual Earnings
Atlanta, GA	$22,106
Chicago, IL	$20,980
Dallas-Fort Worth, TX	$24,445
Denver, CO	$22,591
Los Angeles, CA	$18,923
Minneapolis-St. Paul, MN	$26,166
New York, NY	$20,763
Phoenix, AZ	$20,199
San Francisco, CA	$23,272
Seattle, WA	$25,439

Average Earnings in Most Important Industries

Industry	Average Annual Earnings
Personal and Laundry Services	$20,456

BILL AND ACCOUNT COLLECTORS

- Average Earnings: $28,160
- Beginning Earnings: $19,410
- 25th Percentile: $23,210
- 75th Percentile: $34,670

Average Earnings in Major Metropolitan Areas

Metropolitan Area	Average Annual Earnings
Atlanta, GA	$28,170
Chicago, IL	$29,840
Dallas-Fort Worth, TX	$31,130
Denver, CO	$30,570
Los Angeles, CA	$32,120
Minneapolis-St. Paul, MN	$32,360
New York, NY	$33,730
Phoenix, AZ	$28,370
San Francisco, CA	$38,870

Average Earnings in Most Important Industries

Industry	Average Annual Earnings
Professional, Scientific, and Technical Services	$29,590
Credit Intermediation and Related Activities	$28,820
Ambulatory Health Care Services	$28,720
Hospitals	$27,610
Administrative and Support Services	$25,670

BILLING AND POSTING CLERKS AND MACHINE OPERATORS

- Average Earnings: $27,780
- Beginning Earnings: $19,370
- 25th Percentile: $23,130
- 75th Percentile: $33,790

Average Earnings in Major Metropolitan Areas

Metropolitan Area	Average Annual Earnings
Atlanta, GA	$29,890
Chicago, IL	$29,560
Dallas-Fort Worth, TX	$28,690
Denver, CO	$31,260
Los Angeles, CA	$29,780
Minneapolis-St. Paul, MN	$32,400
New York, NY	$33,530
Phoenix, AZ	$29,370
San Francisco, CA	$36,070
Seattle, WA	$32,820

Average Earnings in Most Important Industries

Industry	Average Annual Earnings
Professional, Scientific, and Technical Services	$28,560
Ambulatory Health Care Services	$27,980
Hospitals	$27,430
Merchant Wholesalers, Durable Goods	$27,430
Administrative and Support Services	$26,800

BIOLOGICAL SCIENTISTS

- Average Earnings: $60,280
- Beginning Earnings: $34,907
- 25th Percentile: $45,293
- 75th Percentile: $78,756

Average Earnings in Major Metropolitan Areas

Metropolitan Area	Average Annual Earnings
Atlanta, GA	$64,597
Chicago, IL	$58,745
Dallas-Fort Worth, TX	$59,117
Denver, CO	$65,946
Los Angeles, CA	$54,193
Minneapolis-St. Paul, MN	$56,201
New York, NY	$65,371
Phoenix, AZ	$49,205
San Francisco, CA	$71,468
Seattle, WA	$57,555

Average Earnings in Most Important Industries

Industry	Average Annual Earnings
Chemical Manufacturing	$66,898
Professional, Scientific, and Technical Services	$64,530
Federal, State, and Local Government	$59,610
Hospitals	$58,596
Educational Services	$41,987

BOILERMAKERS

- Average Earnings: $48,050
- Beginning Earnings: $30,430
- 25th Percentile: $38,340
- 75th Percentile: $59,840

Average Earnings in Major Metropolitan Areas

Metropolitan Area	Average Annual Earnings
Atlanta, GA	$44,960
Chicago, IL	$67,510
New York, NY	$70,760
San Francisco, CA	$65,380

Average Earnings in Most Important Industries

Industry	Average Annual Earnings
Construction of Buildings	$51,750
Specialty Trade Contractors	$50,300
Heavy and Civil Engineering Construction	$48,040
Repair and Maintenance	$42,770
Fabricated Metal Product Manufacturing	$41,440

BOOKBINDERS AND BINDERY WORKERS

- Average Earnings: $25,492
- Beginning Earnings: $16,285
- 25th Percentile: $19,848
- 75th Percentile: $33,336

Average Earnings in Major Metropolitan Areas

Metropolitan Area	Average Annual Earnings
Atlanta, GA	$26,776
Chicago, IL	$25,920
Dallas-Fort Worth, TX	$22,098
Denver, CO	$25,170
Los Angeles, CA	$22,408
Minneapolis-St. Paul, MN	$30,700
New York, NY	$26,004
Phoenix, AZ	$21,670
San Francisco, CA	$28,538
Seattle, WA	$48,570

Average Earnings in Most Important Industries

Industry	Average Annual Earnings
Publishing Industries (Except Internet)	$26,321
Printing and Related Support Activities	$25,713
Professional, Scientific, and Technical Services	$23,605
Paper Manufacturing	$22,780
Administrative and Support Services	$19,990

BOOKKEEPING, ACCOUNTING, AND AUDITING CLERKS

- Average Earnings: $29,490
- Beginning Earnings: $19,030
- 25th Percentile: $23,620
- 75th Percentile: $36,360

Average Earnings in Major Metropolitan Areas

Metropolitan Area	Average Annual Earnings
Atlanta, GA	$30,300
Chicago, IL	$31,090
Dallas-Fort Worth, TX	$30,720
Denver, CO	$33,380
Los Angeles, CA	$33,160
Minneapolis-St. Paul, MN	$33,040
New York, NY	$35,110
Phoenix, AZ	$29,480
San Francisco, CA	$38,100
Seattle, WA	$33,410

Average Earnings in Most Important Industries

Industry	Average Annual Earnings
Federal, State, and Local Government	$31,370
Specialty Trade Contractors	$31,040
Professional, Scientific, and Technical Services	$30,880
Educational Services	$30,500
Administrative and Support Services	$28,210

BRICKMASONS, BLOCKMASONS, AND STONEMASONS

- Average Earnings: $40,935
- Beginning Earnings: $23,494
- 25th Percentile: $31,229
- 75th Percentile: $51,747

Average Earnings in Major Metropolitan Areas

Metropolitan Area	Average Annual Earnings
Atlanta, GA	$37,250
Chicago, IL	$61,140
Dallas-Fort Worth, TX	$37,464
Denver, CO	$50,730
Los Angeles, CA	$38,310
Minneapolis-St. Paul, MN	$55,590
New York, NY	$47,597
Phoenix, AZ	$33,879
San Francisco, CA	$60,856
Seattle, WA	$56,540

Average Earnings in Most Important Industries

Industry	Average Annual Earnings
Primary Metal Manufacturing	$52,920
Construction of Buildings	$41,372
Specialty Trade Contractors	$40,962
Heavy and Civil Engineering Construction	$40,914
Administrative and Support Services	$36,499

BROADCAST AND SOUND ENGINEERING TECHNICIANS AND RADIO OPERATORS

- Average Earnings: $32,884
- Beginning Earnings: $18,027
- 25th Percentile: $23,793
- 75th Percentile: $46,875

Average Earnings in Major Metropolitan Areas

Metropolitan Area	Average Annual Earnings
Atlanta, GA	$35,120
Chicago, IL	$30,389
Dallas-Fort Worth, TX	$27,110
Denver, CO	$34,782
Los Angeles, CA	$36,772
Minneapolis-St. Paul, MN	$37,425
New York, NY	$37,000
Phoenix, AZ	$27,538
San Francisco, CA	$36,284
Seattle, WA	$34,765

Average Earnings in Most Important Industries

Industry	Average Annual Earnings
Motion Picture and Sound Recording Industries	$37,955
Educational Services	$34,152
Rental and Leasing Services	$33,669
Performing Arts, Spectator Sports, and Related Industries	$31,117
Broadcasting (Except Internet)	$28,693

BROKERAGE CLERKS

- Average Earnings: $35,450
- Beginning Earnings: $23,950
- 25th Percentile: $28,780
- 75th Percentile: $44,850

Average Earnings in Major Metropolitan Areas

Metropolitan Area	Average Annual Earnings
Atlanta, GA	$27,650
Dallas-Fort Worth, TX	$40,470
Denver, CO	$38,790
Los Angeles, CA	$40,710
Minneapolis-St. Paul, MN	$33,850
New York, NY	$41,360
Phoenix, AZ	$32,470
San Francisco, CA	$43,710
Seattle, WA	$37,330

Average Earnings in Most Important Industries

Industry	Average Annual Earnings
Securities, Commodity Contracts, and Other Financial Investments and Related Activities	$36,620
Credit Intermediation and Related Activities	$33,660
Administrative and Support Services	$33,530
Insurance Carriers and Related Activities	$31,950
Management of Companies and Enterprises	$31,080

BUDGET ANALYSTS

- Average Earnings: $58,910
- Beginning Earnings: $38,720
- 25th Percentile: $47,530
- 75th Percentile: $73,880

Average Earnings in Major Metropolitan Areas

Metropolitan Area	Average Annual Earnings
Atlanta, GA	$56,140
Chicago, IL	$62,520
Dallas-Fort Worth, TX	$58,400
Denver, CO	$63,770
Los Angeles, CA	$67,690
Minneapolis-St. Paul, MN	$55,500
New York, NY	$67,050
Phoenix, AZ	$54,870
San Francisco, CA	$74,880
Seattle, WA	$62,690

Average Earnings in Most Important Industries

Industry	Average Annual Earnings
Computer and Electronic Product Manufacturing	$72,860
Professional, Scientific, and Technical Services	$64,080
Management of Companies and Enterprises	$63,070
Federal, State, and Local Government	$58,450
Educational Services	$49,620

BUILDING CLEANING WORKERS

- Average Earnings: $19,384
- Beginning Earnings: $13,649
- 25th Percentile: $15,897
- 75th Percentile: $24,769

Average Earnings in Major Metropolitan Areas

Metropolitan Area	Average Annual Earnings
Atlanta, GA	$19,213
Chicago, IL	$20,784
Dallas-Fort Worth, TX	$17,416
Denver, CO	$19,992
Los Angeles, CA	$19,549
Minneapolis-St. Paul, MN	$22,032
New York, NY	$25,239
Phoenix, AZ	$17,319
San Francisco, CA	$24,371
Seattle, WA	$24,030

Average Earnings in Most Important Industries

Industry	Average Annual Earnings
Educational Services	$23,688
Hospitals	$20,520
Nursing and Residential Care Facilities	$18,641
Administrative and Support Services	$17,936
Accommodation	$17,316

BUS DRIVERS

- Average Earnings: $26,031
- Beginning Earnings: $14,913
- 25th Percentile: $19,606
- 75th Percentile: $32,800

Average Earnings in Major Metropolitan Areas

Metropolitan Area	Average Annual Earnings
Atlanta, GA	$21,220
Chicago, IL	$25,950
Dallas-Fort Worth, TX	$22,430
Denver, CO	$30,173
Los Angeles, CA	$30,970
Minneapolis-St. Paul, MN	$28,750
New York, NY	$34,362
Phoenix, AZ	$23,858
San Francisco, CA	$29,720
Seattle, WA	$32,020

Average Earnings in Most Important Industries

Industry	Average Annual Earnings
Federal, State, and Local Government	$33,562
Transit and Ground Passenger Transportation	$25,465
Rental and Leasing Services	$24,390
Educational Services	$23,587
Social Assistance	$19,169

CARDIOVASCULAR TECHNOLOGISTS AND TECHNICIANS

- Average Earnings: $40,420
- Beginning Earnings: $22,810
- 25th Percentile: $28,930
- 75th Percentile: $52,480

Average Earnings in Major Metropolitan Areas

Metropolitan Area	Average Annual Earnings
Atlanta, GA	$34,560
Chicago, IL	$35,920
Dallas-Fort Worth, TX	$39,380
Denver, CO	$40,420
Los Angeles, CA	$45,980
Minneapolis-St. Paul, MN	$40,020
New York, NY	$48,170
Phoenix, AZ	$34,120
San Francisco, CA	$51,770
Seattle, WA	$57,420

Average Earnings in Most Important Industries

Industry	Average Annual Earnings
Administrative and Support Services	$59,430
Educational Services	$48,230
Federal, State, and Local Government	$44,260
Ambulatory Health Care Services	$40,590
Hospitals	$39,540

CARGO AND FREIGHT AGENTS

- Average Earnings: $35,860
- Beginning Earnings: $21,630
- 25th Percentile: $26,730
- 75th Percentile: $45,040

Average Earnings in Major Metropolitan Areas

Metropolitan Area	Average Annual Earnings
Atlanta, GA	$37,000
Chicago, IL	$38,940
Dallas-Fort Worth, TX	$31,480
Denver, CO	$29,010
Los Angeles, CA	$47,430
Minneapolis-St. Paul, MN	$38,590
New York, NY	$37,300
San Francisco, CA	$36,950
Seattle, WA	$44,970

Average Earnings in Most Important Industries

Industry	Average Annual Earnings
Air Transportation	$37,390
Support Activities for Transportation	$35,270
Couriers and Messengers	$34,790
Truck Transportation	$34,470
Warehousing and Storage	$30,690

CARPENTERS

- Average Earnings: $35,580
- Beginning Earnings: $21,940
- 25th Percentile: $27,450
- 75th Percentile: $48,120

Average Earnings in Major Metropolitan Areas

Metropolitan Area	Average Annual Earnings
Atlanta, GA	$32,140
Chicago, IL	$53,590
Dallas-Fort Worth, TX	$26,880
Denver, CO	$38,080
Los Angeles, CA	$46,690
Minneapolis-St. Paul, MN	$44,490
New York, NY	$48,260
Phoenix, AZ	$33,040
San Francisco, CA	$53,730
Seattle, WA	$46,630

Average Earnings in Most Important Industries

Industry	Average Annual Earnings
Heavy and Civil Engineering Construction	$38,090
Construction of Buildings	$36,210
Specialty Trade Contractors	$35,700
Administrative and Support Services	$33,330
Wood Product Manufacturing	$28,230

CARPET, FLOOR, AND TILE INSTALLERS AND FINISHERS

- Average Earnings: $34,470
- Beginning Earnings: $20,094
- 25th Percentile: $25,886
- 75th Percentile: $46,644

Average Earnings in Major Metropolitan Areas

Metropolitan Area	Average Annual Earnings
Chicago, IL	$62,361
Dallas-Fort Worth, TX	$29,480
Denver, CO	$40,403
Los Angeles, CA	$36,790
Minneapolis-St. Paul, MN	$45,566
New York, NY	$42,865
Phoenix, AZ	$27,488
San Francisco, CA	$38,505
Seattle, WA	$48,942

Average Earnings in Most Important Industries

Industry	Average Annual Earnings
Specialty Trade Contractors	$35,817
Furniture and Home Furnishings Stores	$31,310

CASHIERS

- Average Earnings: $16,291
- Beginning Earnings: $12,456
- 25th Percentile: $14,061
- 75th Percentile: $19,120

Average Earnings in Major Metropolitan Areas

Metropolitan Area	Average Annual Earnings
Atlanta, GA	$16,300
Chicago, IL	$16,634
Dallas-Fort Worth, TX	$16,359
Denver, CO	$19,136
Los Angeles, CA	$17,486
Minneapolis-St. Paul, MN	$17,800
New York, NY	$16,430
Phoenix, AZ	$17,268
San Francisco, CA	$20,130
Seattle, WA	$21,210

Average Earnings in Most Important Industries

Industry	Average Annual Earnings
Food and Beverage Stores	$16,410
General Merchandise Stores	$16,290
Health and Personal Care Stores	$16,250
Gasoline Stations	$15,770
Food Services and Drinking Places	$15,060

CEMENT MASONS, CONCRETE FINISHERS, SEGMENTAL PAVERS, AND TERRAZZO WORKERS

- Average Earnings: $32,019
- Beginning Earnings: $20,093
- 25th Percentile: $24,890
- 75th Percentile: $42,236

Average Earnings in Major Metropolitan Areas

Metropolitan Area	Average Annual Earnings
Atlanta, GA	$29,020
Chicago, IL	$48,235
Dallas-Fort Worth, TX	$27,570
Denver, CO	$33,240
Los Angeles, CA	$40,510
Minneapolis-St. Paul, MN	$44,160
New York, NY	$47,060
Phoenix, AZ	$32,070
San Francisco, CA	$48,430
Seattle, WA	$34,170

Average Earnings in Most Important Industries

Industry	Average Annual Earnings
Construction of Buildings	$32,867
Specialty Trade Contractors	$32,159
Heavy and Civil Engineering Construction	$31,843
Administrative and Support Services	$28,260
Nonmetallic Mineral Product Manufacturing	$25,683

CHEFS, COOKS, AND FOOD PREPARATION WORKERS

- Average Earnings: $18,305
- Beginning Earnings: $13,237
- 25th Percentile: $15,289
- 75th Percentile: $22,172

Average Earnings in Major Metropolitan Areas

Metropolitan Area	Average Annual Earnings
Atlanta, GA	$16,906
Chicago, IL	$17,743
Dallas-Fort Worth, TX	$17,226
Denver, CO	$20,434
Los Angeles, CA	$19,069
Minneapolis-St. Paul, MN	$21,570
New York, NY	$22,117
Phoenix, AZ	$18,727
San Francisco, CA	$21,686
Seattle, WA	$22,659

Average Earnings in Most Important Industries

Industry	Average Annual Earnings
Accommodation	$23,402
Food Services and Drinking Places	$17,791
Nursing and Residential Care Facilities	$18,711
Educational Services	$18,599
Food and Beverage Stores	$18,159

CHEMISTS AND MATERIALS SCIENTISTS

- Average Earnings: $59,156
- Beginning Earnings: $35,276
- 25th Percentile: $44,432
- 75th Percentile: $80,423

Average Earnings in Major Metropolitan Areas

Metropolitan Area	Average Annual Earnings
Atlanta, GA	$52,650
Chicago, IL	$52,980
Dallas-Fort Worth, TX	$63,214
Denver, CO	$66,192
Los Angeles, CA	$54,336
Minneapolis-St. Paul, MN	$67,796
New York, NY	$61,956
Phoenix, AZ	$50,530
San Francisco, CA	$63,795
Seattle, WA	$51,030

Average Earnings in Most Important Industries

Industry	Average Annual Earnings
Federal, State, and Local Government	$68,291
Management of Companies and Enterprises	$68,265
Chemical Manufacturing	$58,900
Professional, Scientific, and Technical Services	$57,547
Educational Services	$42,654

CHILD CARE WORKERS

- Average Earnings: $17,050
- Beginning Earnings: $12,540
- 25th Percentile: $14,320
- 75th Percentile: $21,250

Average Earnings in Major Metropolitan Areas

Metropolitan Area	Average Annual Earnings
Atlanta, GA	$16,120
Chicago, IL	$19,200
Dallas-Fort Worth, TX	$14,680
Denver, CO	$19,340
Los Angeles, CA	$19,900
Minneapolis-St. Paul, MN	$17,780
New York, NY	$22,400
Phoenix, AZ	$15,940
San Francisco, CA	$23,470
Seattle, WA	$18,410

Average Earnings in Most Important Industries

Industry	Average Annual Earnings
Nursing and Residential Care Facilities	$20,270
Educational Services	$19,830
Religious, Grantmaking, Civic, Professional, and Similar Organizations	$16,390
Amusement, Gambling, and Recreation Industries	$16,050
Social Assistance	$15,960

CHIROPRACTORS

- Average Earnings: $67,200
- Beginning Earnings: $32,900
- 25th Percentile: $46,170
- 75th Percentile: $102,920

Average Earnings in Major Metropolitan Areas

Metropolitan Area	Average Annual Earnings
Chicago, IL	$66,150
Dallas-Fort Worth, TX	$41,750
Los Angeles, CA	$47,760
Minneapolis-St. Paul, MN	$73,970
New York, NY	$69,460
Phoenix, AZ	$100,530
San Francisco, CA	$74,110

Average Earnings in Most Important Industries

Industry	Average Annual Earnings
Ambulatory Health Care Services	$67,700

CLAIMS ADJUSTERS, APPRAISERS, EXAMINERS, AND INVESTIGATORS

- Average Earnings: $46,289
- Beginning Earnings: $28,898
- 25th Percentile: $35,987
- 75th Percentile: $59,597

Average Earnings in Major Metropolitan Areas

Metropolitan Area	Average Annual Earnings
Atlanta, GA	$49,186
Chicago, IL	$46,414
Dallas-Fort Worth, TX	$47,669
Denver, CO	$48,180
Los Angeles, CA	$54,329
Minneapolis-St. Paul, MN	$42,483
New York, NY	$53,330
Phoenix, AZ	$46,677
San Francisco, CA	$56,378
Seattle, WA	$51,840

Average Earnings in Most Important Industries

Industry	Average Annual Earnings
Insurance Carriers and Related Activities	$46,516

CLINICAL LABORATORY TECHNOLOGISTS AND TECHNICIANS

- Average Earnings: $40,053
- Beginning Earnings: $27,367
- 25th Percentile: $32,983
- 75th Percentile: $48,124

Average Earnings in Major Metropolitan Areas

Metropolitan Area	Average Annual Earnings
Atlanta, GA	$40,065
Chicago, IL	$41,074
Dallas-Fort Worth, TX	$36,740
Denver, CO	$40,740
Los Angeles, CA	$50,080
Minneapolis-St. Paul, MN	$42,496
New York, NY	$46,157
Phoenix, AZ	$36,026
San Francisco, CA	$56,566
Seattle, WA	$44,592

Average Earnings in Most Important Industries

Industry	Average Annual Earnings
Federal, State, and Local Government	$44,650
Hospitals	$41,906
Professional, Scientific, and Technical Services	$39,102
Educational Services	$36,939
Ambulatory Health Care Services	$36,809

COIN, VENDING, AND AMUSEMENT MACHINE SERVICERS AND REPAIRERS

- Average Earnings: $28,200
- Beginning Earnings: $18,100
- 25th Percentile: $22,090
- 75th Percentile: $35,060

Average Earnings in Major Metropolitan Areas

Metropolitan Area	Average Annual Earnings
Atlanta, GA	$29,530
Chicago, IL	$30,040
Dallas-Fort Worth, TX	$25,780
Denver, CO	$34,860
Los Angeles, CA	$28,850
Minneapolis-St. Paul, MN	$36,590
New York, NY	$29,310
Phoenix, AZ	$30,850
San Francisco, CA	$29,930
Seattle, WA	$33,320

Average Earnings in Most Important Industries

Industry	Average Annual Earnings
Accommodation	$34,730
Beverage and Tobacco Product Manufacturing	$31,670
Merchant Wholesalers, Nondurable Goods	$30,540
Amusement, Gambling, and Recreation Industries	$26,160
Nonstore Retailers	$26,090

COMMERCIAL AND INDUSTRIAL DESIGNERS

- Average Earnings: $52,200
- Beginning Earnings: $29,720
- 25th Percentile: $39,220
- 75th Percentile: $70,260

Average Earnings in Major Metropolitan Areas

Metropolitan Area	Average Annual Earnings
Atlanta, GA	$47,700
Chicago, IL	$51,910
Dallas-Fort Worth, TX	$51,430
Denver, CO	$48,640
Los Angeles, CA	$55,750
Minneapolis-St. Paul, MN	$52,310
New York, NY	$51,560
Phoenix, AZ	$49,490
San Francisco, CA	$57,150
Seattle, WA	$51,030

Average Earnings in Most Important Industries

Industry	Average Annual Earnings
Transportation Equipment Manufacturing	$61,210
Professional, Scientific, and Technical Services	$57,220
Machinery Manufacturing	$50,850
Merchant Wholesalers, Durable Goods	$48,930
Miscellaneous Manufacturing	$43,560

COMMUNICATIONS EQUIPMENT OPERATORS

- Average Earnings: $23,434
- Beginning Earnings: $15,867
- 25th Percentile: $19,121
- 75th Percentile: $28,907

Average Earnings in Major Metropolitan Areas

Metropolitan Area	Average Annual Earnings
Atlanta, GA	$24,643
Chicago, IL	$24,783
Dallas-Fort Worth, TX	$22,060
Denver, CO	$23,340
Los Angeles, CA	$23,393
Minneapolis-St. Paul, MN	$24,660
New York, NY	$29,012
Phoenix, AZ	$21,970
San Francisco, CA	$31,130
Seattle, WA	$25,640

Average Earnings in Most Important Industries

Industry	Average Annual Earnings
Telecommunications	$34,828
Ambulatory Health Care Services	$22,926
Hospitals	$22,743
Motor Vehicle and Parts Dealers	$20,413
Administrative and Support Services	$20,229

COMPUTER AND INFORMATION SYSTEMS MANAGERS

- Average Earnings: $96,520
- Beginning Earnings: $57,300
- 25th Percentile: $75,240
- 75th Percentile: $123,140

Average Earnings in Major Metropolitan Areas

Metropolitan Area	Average Annual Earnings
Atlanta, GA	$97,990
Chicago, IL	$87,950
Dallas-Fort Worth, TX	$102,860
Denver, CO	$103,060
Los Angeles, CA	$108,460
Minneapolis-St. Paul, MN	$101,770
New York, NY	$123,020
Phoenix, AZ	$87,420
San Francisco, CA	$120,530
Seattle, WA	$105,400

Average Earnings in Most Important Industries

Industry	Average Annual Earnings
Professional, Scientific, and Technical Services	$103,980
Management of Companies and Enterprises	$102,480
Insurance Carriers and Related Activities	$99,260
Federal, State, and Local Government	$84,660
Educational Services	$78,870

COMPUTER CONTROL PROGRAMMERS AND OPERATORS

- Average Earnings: $32,262
- Beginning Earnings: $20,781
- 25th Percentile: $25,480
- 75th Percentile: $40,153

Average Earnings in Major Metropolitan Areas

Metropolitan Area	Average Annual Earnings
Atlanta, GA	$32,760
Chicago, IL	$33,348
Dallas-Fort Worth, TX	$30,515
Denver, CO	$32,852
Los Angeles, CA	$33,739
Minneapolis-St. Paul, MN	$38,717
New York, NY	$35,323
Phoenix, AZ	$32,617
San Francisco, CA	$36,430
Seattle, WA	$45,380

Average Earnings in Most Important Industries

Industry	Average Annual Earnings
Machinery Manufacturing	$35,234
Fabricated Metal Product Manufacturing	$32,458
Transportation Equipment Manufacturing	$30,592
Computer and Electronic Product Manufacturing	$28,799
Plastics and Rubber Products Manufacturing	$25,841

COMPUTER OPERATORS

- Average Earnings: $32,070
- Beginning Earnings: $19,710
- 25th Percentile: $24,740
- 75th Percentile: $41,330

Average Earnings in Major Metropolitan Areas

Metropolitan Area	Average Annual Earnings
Atlanta, GA	$34,280
Chicago, IL	$34,550
Dallas-Fort Worth, TX	$33,630
Denver, CO	$37,860
Los Angeles, CA	$32,530
Minneapolis-St. Paul, MN	$34,150
New York, NY	$36,620
Phoenix, AZ	$30,010
San Francisco, CA	$39,840
Seattle, WA	$37,760

Average Earnings in Most Important Industries

Industry	Average Annual Earnings
Federal, State, and Local Government	$35,410
Professional, Scientific, and Technical Services	$32,270
Educational Services	$31,520
Administrative and Support Services	$29,930
Credit Intermediation and Related Activities	$27,900

COMPUTER PROGRAMMERS

- Average Earnings: $63,420
- Beginning Earnings: $37,380
- 25th Percentile: $48,040
- 75th Percentile: $82,600

Average Earnings in Major Metropolitan Areas

Metropolitan Area	Average Annual Earnings
Atlanta, GA	$67,290
Chicago, IL	$62,940
Dallas-Fort Worth, TX	$70,910
Denver, CO	$70,420
Los Angeles, CA	$69,770
Minneapolis-St. Paul, MN	$66,110
New York, NY	$72,020
Phoenix, AZ	$59,000
San Francisco, CA	$75,820

Average Earnings in Most Important Industries

Industry	Average Annual Earnings
Publishing Industries (Except Internet)	$74,010
Merchant Wholesalers, Durable Goods	$69,740
Administrative and Support Services	$65,290
Professional, Scientific, and Technical Services	$64,880
Insurance Carriers and Related Activities	$64,480

COMPUTER SCIENTISTS AND DATABASE ADMINISTRATORS

- Average Earnings: $64,395
- Beginning Earnings: $34,528
- 25th Percentile: $46,827
- 75th Percentile: $85,128

Average Earnings in Major Metropolitan Areas

Metropolitan Area	Average Annual Earnings
Atlanta, GA	$59,977
Chicago, IL	$66,619
Dallas-Fort Worth, TX	$66,452
Denver, CO	$65,181
Los Angeles, CA	$70,465
Minneapolis-St. Paul, MN	$65,028
New York, NY	$72,970
Phoenix, AZ	$52,423
San Francisco, CA	$85,207
Seattle, WA	$71,650

Average Earnings in Most Important Industries

Industry	Average Annual Earnings
Publishing Industries (Except Internet)	$72,364
Professional, Scientific, and Technical Services	$70,821
Management of Companies and Enterprises	$66,232
Federal, State, and Local Government	$64,124
Educational Services	$49,319

COMPUTER SOFTWARE ENGINEERS

- Average Earnings: $79,167
- Beginning Earnings: $49,236
- 25th Percentile: $62,340
- 75th Percentile: $97,782

Average Earnings in Major Metropolitan Areas

Metropolitan Area	Average Annual Earnings
Atlanta, GA	$72,836
Chicago, IL	$77,441
Dallas-Fort Worth, TX	$74,800
Denver, CO	$82,326
Los Angeles, CA	$81,813
Minneapolis-St. Paul, MN	$76,857
New York, NY	$88,371
Phoenix, AZ	$71,742
San Francisco, CA	$91,199
Seattle, WA	$80,220

Average Earnings in Most Important Industries

Industry	Average Annual Earnings
Computer and Electronic Product Manufacturing	$86,572
Publishing Industries (Except Internet)	$81,789
Professional, Scientific, and Technical Services	$79,735
Telecommunications	$77,976
Internet Service Providers, Web Search Portals, and Data Processing Service	$76,509

COMPUTER SUPPORT SPECIALISTS AND SYSTEMS ADMINISTRATORS

- Average Earnings: $50,174
- Beginning Earnings: $30,523
- 25th Percentile: $38,813
- 75th Percentile: $64,791

Average Earnings in Major Metropolitan Areas

Metropolitan Area	Average Annual Earnings
Atlanta, GA	$50,195
Chicago, IL	$52,743
Dallas-Fort Worth, TX	$52,590
Denver, CO	$58,892
Los Angeles, CA	$51,589
Minneapolis-St. Paul, MN	$55,641
New York, NY	$61,406
Phoenix, AZ	$47,747
San Francisco, CA	$64,524
Seattle, WA	$59,153

Average Earnings in Most Important Industries

Industry	Average Annual Earnings
Management of Companies and Enterprises	$54,738
Professional, Scientific, and Technical Services	$52,825
Federal, State, and Local Government	$48,274
Administrative and Support Services	$43,379
Educational Services	$42,651

COMPUTER SYSTEMS ANALYSTS

- Average Earnings: $68,300
- Beginning Earnings: $43,080
- 25th Percentile: $54,070
- 75th Percentile: $85,210

Average Earnings in Major Metropolitan Areas

Metropolitan Area	Average Annual Earnings
Atlanta, GA	$73,500
Chicago, IL	$73,460
Dallas-Fort Worth, TX	$74,010
Denver, CO	$72,490
Los Angeles, CA	$69,270
Minneapolis-St. Paul, MN	$67,670
New York, NY	$75,520
Phoenix, AZ	$65,670
San Francisco, CA	$79,470
Seattle, WA	$72,860

Average Earnings in Most Important Industries

Industry	Average Annual Earnings
Merchant Wholesalers, Durable Goods	$74,710
Professional, Scientific, and Technical Services	$69,550
Management of Companies and Enterprises	$69,020
Federal, State, and Local Government	$68,710
Insurance Carriers and Related Activities	$68,250

COMPUTER, AUTOMATED TELLER, AND OFFICE MACHINE REPAIRERS

- Average Earnings: $36,060
- Beginning Earnings: $22,370
- 25th Percentile: $28,290
- 75th Percentile: $45,590

Average Earnings in Major Metropolitan Areas

Metropolitan Area	Average Annual Earnings
Atlanta, GA	$35,630
Chicago, IL	$38,240
Dallas-Fort Worth, TX	$33,920
Denver, CO	$41,940
Los Angeles, CA	$36,600
Minneapolis-St. Paul, MN	$38,050
New York, NY	$43,060
Phoenix, AZ	$36,140
San Francisco, CA	$44,040
Seattle, WA	$35,830

Average Earnings in Most Important Industries

Industry	Average Annual Earnings
Professional, Scientific, and Technical Services	$39,460
Merchant Wholesalers, Durable Goods	$38,960
Miscellaneous Store Retailers	$33,140
Repair and Maintenance	$32,930
Electronics and Appliance Stores	$31,270

CONSERVATION SCIENTISTS AND FORESTERS

- Average Earnings: $51,436
- Beginning Earnings: $30,885
- 25th Percentile: $39,214
- 75th Percentile: $64,793

Average Earnings in Major Metropolitan Areas

Metropolitan Area	Average Annual Earnings
Atlanta, GA	$66,585
Chicago, IL	$60,585
Dallas-Fort Worth, TX	$66,730
Denver, CO	$56,012
Los Angeles, CA	$64,914
Minneapolis-St. Paul, MN	$56,282
New York, NY	$45,390
Phoenix, AZ	$50,613
San Francisco, CA	$63,650
Seattle, WA	$62,933

Average Earnings in Most Important Industries

Industry	Average Annual Earnings
Federal, State, and Local Government	$52,558

CONSTRUCTION AND BUILDING INSPECTORS

- Average Earnings: $44,720
- Beginning Earnings: $28,390
- 25th Percentile: $35,400
- 75th Percentile: $56,350

Average Earnings in Major Metropolitan Areas

Metropolitan Area	Average Annual Earnings
Atlanta, GA	$41,020
Chicago, IL	$53,840
Dallas-Fort Worth, TX	$43,960
Denver, CO	$50,890
Los Angeles, CA	$63,640
Minneapolis-St. Paul, MN	$54,630
New York, NY	$50,670
Phoenix, AZ	$45,720
San Francisco, CA	$69,480
Seattle, WA	$56,340

Average Earnings in Most Important Industries

Industry	Average Annual Earnings
Construction of Buildings	$46,840
Professional, Scientific, and Technical Services	$45,690
Heavy and Civil Engineering Construction	$45,570
Specialty Trade Contractors	$44,230
Federal, State, and Local Government	$44,050

CONSTRUCTION EQUIPMENT OPERATORS

- Average Earnings: $35,179
- Beginning Earnings: $22,800
- 25th Percentile: $27,473
- 75th Percentile: $46,949

Average Earnings in Major Metropolitan Areas

Metropolitan Area	Average Annual Earnings
Atlanta, GA	$32,421
Chicago, IL	$59,875
Dallas-Fort Worth, TX	$28,467
Denver, CO	$39,082
Los Angeles, CA	$59,175
Minneapolis-St. Paul, MN	$50,520
New York, NY	$60,533
Phoenix, AZ	$38,109
San Francisco, CA	$64,459
Seattle, WA	$55,415

Average Earnings in Most Important Industries

Industry	Average Annual Earnings
Construction of Buildings	$38,451
Heavy and Civil Engineering Construction	$37,695
Specialty Trade Contractors	$36,056
Mining (Except Oil and Gas)	$35,403
Federal, State, and Local Government	$31,532

CONSTRUCTION LABORERS

- Average Earnings: $25,410
- Beginning Earnings: $16,420
- 25th Percentile: $19,920
- 75th Percentile: $35,150

Average Earnings in Major Metropolitan Areas

Metropolitan Area	Average Annual Earnings
Atlanta, GA	$22,690
Chicago, IL	$49,070
Dallas-Fort Worth, TX	$20,960
Denver, CO	$26,290
Los Angeles, CA	$27,720
Minneapolis-St. Paul, MN	$47,920
New York, NY	$44,250
Phoenix, AZ	$24,580
San Francisco, CA	$43,740
Seattle, WA	$32,020

Average Earnings in Most Important Industries

Industry	Average Annual Earnings
Federal, State, and Local Government	$27,630
Heavy and Civil Engineering Construction	$26,510
Construction of Buildings	$26,330
Specialty Trade Contractors	$25,320
Administrative and Support Services	$20,010

CONSTRUCTION MANAGERS

- Average Earnings: $72,260
- Beginning Earnings: $42,900
- 25th Percentile: $55,010
- 75th Percentile: $96,300

Average Earnings in Major Metropolitan Areas

Metropolitan Area	Average Annual Earnings
Atlanta, GA	$69,330
Chicago, IL	$80,710
Dallas-Fort Worth, TX	$59,680
Denver, CO	$72,150
Los Angeles, CA	$87,550
Minneapolis-St. Paul, MN	$85,880
New York, NY	$104,170
Phoenix, AZ	$67,470
San Francisco, CA	$96,640
Seattle, WA	$100,560

Average Earnings in Most Important Industries

Industry	Average Annual Earnings
Professional, Scientific, and Technical Services	$76,460
Heavy and Civil Engineering Construction	$74,450
Specialty Trade Contractors	$72,930
Construction of Buildings	$70,690
Federal, State, and Local Government	$64,300

CORRECTIONAL OFFICERS

- Average Earnings: $35,246
- Beginning Earnings: $23,415
- 25th Percentile: $27,720
- 75th Percentile: $46,271

Average Earnings in Major Metropolitan Areas

Metropolitan Area	Average Annual Earnings
Atlanta, GA	$28,360
Chicago, IL	$55,120
Dallas-Fort Worth, TX	$31,163
Denver, CO	$42,028
Minneapolis-St. Paul, MN	$41,298
New York, NY	$51,937
Phoenix, AZ	$32,366
San Francisco, CA	$57,830

Average Earnings in Most Important Industries

Industry	Average Annual Earnings
Federal, State, and Local Government	$35,537

COST ESTIMATORS

- Average Earnings: $52,020
- Beginning Earnings: $31,200
- 25th Percentile: $39,950
- 75th Percentile: $68,260

Average Earnings in Major Metropolitan Areas

Metropolitan Area	Average Annual Earnings
Atlanta, GA	$48,280
Chicago, IL	$61,560
Dallas-Fort Worth, TX	$52,910
Denver, CO	$55,550
Los Angeles, CA	$56,310
Minneapolis-St. Paul, MN	$56,150
New York, NY	$65,590
Phoenix, AZ	$50,420
San Francisco, CA	$66,700
Seattle, WA	$58,320

Average Earnings in Most Important Industries

Industry	Average Annual Earnings
Heavy and Civil Engineering Construction	$57,420
Construction of Buildings	$55,720
Specialty Trade Contractors	$52,740
Fabricated Metal Product Manufacturing	$48,720
Repair and Maintenance	$44,530

COUNSELORS

- Average Earnings: $37,996
- Beginning Earnings: $23,305
- 25th Percentile: $29,417
- 75th Percentile: $48,924

Average Earnings in Major Metropolitan Areas

Metropolitan Area	Average Annual Earnings
Atlanta, GA	$46,365
Chicago, IL	$45,852
Dallas-Fort Worth, TX	$48,844
Denver, CO	$35,330
Los Angeles, CA	$38,083
Minneapolis-St. Paul, MN	$38,140
New York, NY	$42,365
Phoenix, AZ	$33,640
San Francisco, CA	$43,820
Seattle, WA	$41,807

Average Earnings in Most Important Industries

Industry	Average Annual Earnings
Educational Services	$48,998
Federal, State, and Local Government	$40,463
Ambulatory Health Care Services	$34,569
Social Assistance	$29,842
Nursing and Residential Care Facilities	$26,275

COUNTER AND RENTAL CLERKS

- Average Earnings: $18,970
- Beginning Earnings: $13,170
- 25th Percentile: $15,390
- 75th Percentile: $26,010

Average Earnings in Major Metropolitan Areas

Metropolitan Area	Average Annual Earnings
Atlanta, GA	$20,600
Chicago, IL	$20,320
Dallas-Fort Worth, TX	$23,110
Denver, CO	$19,560
Los Angeles, CA	$19,690
Minneapolis-St. Paul, MN	$17,940
New York, NY	$18,330
Phoenix, AZ	$19,530
San Francisco, CA	$20,330
Seattle, WA	$22,050

Average Earnings in Most Important Industries

Industry	Average Annual Earnings
Motor Vehicle and Parts Dealers	$31,750
Merchant Wholesalers, Durable Goods	$26,860
Rental and Leasing Services	$18,350
Amusement, Gambling, and Recreation Industries	$16,200
Personal and Laundry Services	$16,010

COURIERS AND MESSENGERS

- Average Earnings: $20,870
- Beginning Earnings: $14,330
- 25th Percentile: $16,830
- 75th Percentile: $26,230

Average Earnings in Major Metropolitan Areas

Metropolitan Area	Average Annual Earnings
Atlanta, GA	$23,340
Chicago, IL	$20,240
Dallas-Fort Worth, TX	$25,030
Denver, CO	$25,760
Los Angeles, CA	$17,860
Minneapolis-St. Paul, MN	$29,830
New York, NY	$20,880
Phoenix, AZ	$21,870
Seattle, WA	$23,610

Average Earnings in Most Important Industries

Industry	Average Annual Earnings
Ambulatory Health Care Services	$21,900
Hospitals	$21,710
Credit Intermediation and Related Activities	$20,260
Couriers and Messengers	$20,120
Professional, Scientific, and Technical Services	$19,980

COURT REPORTERS

- Average Earnings: $41,640
- Beginning Earnings: $20,370
- 25th Percentile: $29,830
- 75th Percentile: $56,870

Average Earnings in Major Metropolitan Areas

Metropolitan Area	Average Annual Earnings
Atlanta, GA	$41,810
Chicago, IL	$36,730
New York, NY	$53,230

Average Earnings in Most Important Industries

Industry	Average Annual Earnings
Federal, State, and Local Government	$46,090
Administrative and Support Services	$34,570

CREDIT AUTHORIZERS, CHECKERS, AND CLERKS

- Average Earnings: $29,330
- Beginning Earnings: $17,740
- 25th Percentile: $23,120
- 75th Percentile: $36,580

Average Earnings in Major Metropolitan Areas

Metropolitan Area	Average Annual Earnings
Chicago, IL	$37,600
Denver, CO	$27,920
Los Angeles, CA	$33,360
Minneapolis-St. Paul, MN	$39,430
New York, NY	$32,240
Phoenix, AZ	$17,630
San Francisco, CA	$40,790
Seattle, WA	$35,540

Average Earnings in Most Important Industries

Industry	Average Annual Earnings
Merchant Wholesalers, Durable Goods	$33,480
Motor Vehicle and Parts Dealers	$32,060
Management of Companies and Enterprises	$31,060
Credit Intermediation and Related Activities	$29,170
Administrative and Support Services	$23,910

CUSTOMER SERVICE REPRESENTATIVES

- Average Earnings: $27,490
- Beginning Earnings: $17,820
- 25th Percentile: $21,750
- 75th Percentile: $35,160

Average Earnings in Major Metropolitan Areas

Metropolitan Area	Average Annual Earnings
Atlanta, GA	$28,740
Chicago, IL	$31,240
Dallas-Fort Worth, TX	$28,820
Denver, CO	$28,560
Los Angeles, CA	$30,270
Minneapolis-St. Paul, MN	$32,370
New York, NY	$32,590
Phoenix, AZ	$26,730
San Francisco, CA	$34,760
Seattle, WA	$32,310

Average Earnings in Most Important Industries

Industry	Average Annual Earnings
Telecommunications	$31,240
Insurance Carriers and Related Activities	$29,890
Professional, Scientific, and Technical Services	$29,280
Credit Intermediation and Related Activities	$27,410
Administrative and Support Services	$22,950

DANCERS AND CHOREOGRAPHERS

- Average Earnings: $32,950
- Beginning Earnings: $15,480
- 25th Percentile: $20,730
- 75th Percentile: $48,070

Average Earnings in Major Metropolitan Areas

Metropolitan Area	Average Annual Earnings
Chicago, IL	$29,350
Dallas-Fort Worth, TX	$42,750
Los Angeles, CA	$40,390
Minneapolis-St. Paul, MN	$48,970
New York, NY	$58,040
Phoenix, AZ	$38,130
San Francisco, CA	$39,640
Seattle, WA	$46,790

Average Earnings in Most Important Industries

Industry	Average Annual Earnings
Performing Arts, Spectator Sports, and Related Industries	$36,050
Educational Services	$32,760

Note: Averages apply only to Choreographers.

DATA ENTRY AND INFORMATION PROCESSING WORKERS

- Average Earnings: $25,587
- Beginning Earnings: $17,632
- 25th Percentile: $21,168
- 75th Percentile: $30,930

Average Earnings in Major Metropolitan Areas

Metropolitan Area	Average Annual Earnings
Atlanta, GA	$24,554
Chicago, IL	$26,511
Dallas-Fort Worth, TX	$25,188
Denver, CO	$37,290
Los Angeles, CA	$24,040
Minneapolis-St. Paul, MN	$28,696
New York, NY	$29,402
Phoenix, AZ	$25,777
San Francisco, CA	$34,163
Seattle, WA	$28,286

Average Earnings in Most Important Industries

Industry	Average Annual Earnings
Federal, State, and Local Government	$29,138
Educational Services	$26,878
Professional, Scientific, and Technical Services	$26,726
Insurance Carriers and Related Activities	$25,529
Administrative and Support Services	$23,197

DEMONSTRATORS, PRODUCT PROMOTERS, AND MODELS

- Average Earnings: $20,762
- Beginning Earnings: $15,186
- 25th Percentile: $17,182
- 75th Percentile: $26,997

Average Earnings in Major Metropolitan Areas

Metropolitan Area	Average Annual Earnings
Atlanta, GA	$20,270
Chicago, IL	$22,210
Los Angeles, CA	$29,770
Minneapolis-St. Paul, MN	$20,070
New York, NY	$24,830
Phoenix, AZ	$22,460
Seattle, WA	$19,055

Average Earnings in Most Important Industries

Industry	Average Annual Earnings
Merchant Wholesalers, Nondurable Goods	$23,520
Administrative and Support Services	$20,740
General Merchandise Stores	$20,510
Professional, Scientific, and Technical Services	$18,960
Food and Beverage Stores	$17,530

DENTAL ASSISTANTS

- Average Earnings: $29,520
- Beginning Earnings: $19,680
- 25th Percentile: $23,980
- 75th Percentile: $35,190

Average Earnings in Major Metropolitan Areas

Metropolitan Area	Average Annual Earnings
Atlanta, GA	$30,350
Chicago, IL	$30,180
Dallas-Fort Worth, TX	$29,910
Denver, CO	$36,320
Los Angeles, CA	$30,480
Minneapolis-St. Paul, MN	$36,960
New York, NY	$31,800
Phoenix, AZ	$32,610
San Francisco, CA	$37,690
Seattle, WA	$36,070

Average Earnings in Most Important Industries

Industry	Average Annual Earnings
Ambulatory Health Care Services	$29,490

DENTAL HYGIENISTS

- Average Earnings: $60,890
- Beginning Earnings: $38,470
- 25th Percentile: $49,120
- 75th Percentile: $71,480

Average Earnings in Major Metropolitan Areas

Metropolitan Area	Average Annual Earnings
Atlanta, GA	$61,700
Chicago, IL	$64,730
Dallas-Fort Worth, TX	$68,980
Denver, CO	$79,530
Los Angeles, CA	$72,100
Minneapolis-St. Paul, MN	$67,380
New York, NY	$67,670
Phoenix, AZ	$72,230
San Francisco, CA	$87,700
Seattle, WA	$82,680

Average Earnings in Most Important Industries

Industry	Average Annual Earnings
Ambulatory Health Care Services	$61,010

DENTISTS

- Average Earnings: $111,111
- Beginning Earnings: $64,317
- 25th Percentile: $91,470
- 75th Percentile: more than $145,600

Average Earnings in Major Metropolitan Areas

Metropolitan Area	Average Annual Earnings
Atlanta, GA	$145,600
Chicago, IL	$75,120
Dallas-Fort Worth, TX	$145,600
Denver, CO	$145,600
Los Angeles, CA	$113,130
New York, NY	$125,122
Phoenix, AZ	$129,350
San Francisco, CA	$145,600
Seattle, WA	$138,290

Average Earnings in Most Important Industries

Industry	Average Annual Earnings
Ambulatory Health Care Services	$130,945

Note: Median earnings apply only to Dentists, General, and to Dentists, All Other Specialists.

DESKTOP PUBLISHERS

- Average Earnings: $32,800
- Beginning Earnings: $19,190
- 25th Percentile: $24,950
- 75th Percentile: $43,000

Average Earnings in Major Metropolitan Areas

Metropolitan Area	Average Annual Earnings
Atlanta, GA	$31,160
Chicago, IL	$34,810
Dallas-Fort Worth, TX	$28,250
Los Angeles, CA	$34,100
Minneapolis-St. Paul, MN	$43,470
New York, NY	$42,010
Phoenix, AZ	$25,560
San Francisco, CA	$39,410
Seattle, WA	$38,350

Average Earnings in Most Important Industries

Industry	Average Annual Earnings
Management of Companies and Enterprises	$39,860
Printing and Related Support Activities	$35,270
Professional, Scientific, and Technical Services	$34,110
Publishing Industries (Except Internet)	$30,260
Administrative and Support Services	$28,280

DIAGNOSTIC MEDICAL SONOGRAPHERS

- Average Earnings: $54,370
- Beginning Earnings: $38,970
- 25th Percentile: $46,710
- 75th Percentile: $64,330

Average Earnings in Major Metropolitan Areas

Metropolitan Area	Average Annual Earnings
Atlanta, GA	$53,450
Chicago, IL	$56,000
Dallas-Fort Worth, TX	$58,880
Denver, CO	$58,860
Los Angeles, CA	$54,950
Minneapolis-St. Paul, MN	$60,320
New York, NY	$55,820
Phoenix, AZ	$62,090
San Francisco, CA	$69,270
Seattle, WA	$65,820

Average Earnings in Most Important Industries

Industry	Average Annual Earnings
Ambulatory Health Care Services	$54,450
Hospitals	$54,190

DIESEL SERVICE TECHNICIANS AND MECHANICS

- Average Earnings: $36,620
- Beginning Earnings: $23,790
- 25th Percentile: $29,420
- 75th Percentile: $44,410

Average Earnings in Major Metropolitan Areas

Metropolitan Area	Average Annual Earnings
Atlanta, GA	$39,000
Chicago, IL	$42,130
Dallas-Fort Worth, TX	$37,180
Denver, CO	$42,050
Los Angeles, CA	$42,430
Minneapolis-St. Paul, MN	$41,120
New York, NY	$47,390
Phoenix, AZ	$34,820
San Francisco, CA	$51,570
Seattle, WA	$46,810

Average Earnings in Most Important Industries

Industry	Average Annual Earnings
Federal, State, and Local Government	$41,800
Merchant Wholesalers, Durable Goods	$37,690
Repair and Maintenance	$35,080
Truck Transportation	$34,000
Educational Services	$33,560

DIETITIANS AND NUTRITIONISTS

- Average Earnings: $44,940
- Beginning Earnings: $29,050
- 25th Percentile: $36,960
- 75th Percentile: $54,730

Average Earnings in Major Metropolitan Areas

Metropolitan Area	Average Annual Earnings
Atlanta, GA	$42,760
Chicago, IL	$43,870
Dallas-Fort Worth, TX	$46,210
Denver, CO	$33,310
Los Angeles, CA	$51,670
Minneapolis-St. Paul, MN	$47,690
New York, NY	$50,940
Phoenix, AZ	$40,060
San Francisco, CA	$62,130
Seattle, WA	$52,580

Average Earnings in Most Important Industries

Industry	Average Annual Earnings
Ambulatory Health Care Services	$47,470
Hospitals	$45,670
Federal, State, and Local Government	$44,410
Nursing and Residential Care Facilities	$43,790
Personal and Laundry Services	$37,500

DISPATCHERS

- Average Earnings: $30,921
- Beginning Earnings: $19,104
- 25th Percentile: $23,921
- 75th Percentile: $39,791

Average Earnings in Major Metropolitan Areas

Metropolitan Area	Average Annual Earnings
Atlanta, GA	$31,879
Chicago, IL	$36,504
Dallas-Fort Worth, TX	$31,357
Denver, CO	$36,144
Los Angeles, CA	$34,372
Minneapolis-St. Paul, MN	$37,035
New York, NY	$33,566
Phoenix, AZ	$31,926
San Francisco, CA	$43,107
Seattle, WA	$39,744

Average Earnings in Most Important Industries

Industry	Average Annual Earnings
Truck Transportation	$35,130
Federal, State, and Local Government	$30,505
Support Activities for Transportation	$29,660
Administrative and Support Services	$26,042
Transit and Ground Passenger Transportation	$24,922

DRAFTERS

- Average Earnings: $42,221
- Beginning Earnings: $27,291
- 25th Percentile: $33,714
- 75th Percentile: $52,850

Average Earnings in Major Metropolitan Areas

Metropolitan Area	Average Annual Earnings
Atlanta, GA	$43,078
Chicago, IL	$39,172
Dallas-Fort Worth, TX	$43,551
Denver, CO	$46,658
Los Angeles, CA	$45,013
Minneapolis-St. Paul, MN	$48,412
New York, NY	$48,631
Phoenix, AZ	$41,878
San Francisco, CA	$50,658
Seattle, WA	$46,957

Average Earnings in Most Important Industries

Industry	Average Annual Earnings
Computer and Electronic Product Manufacturing	$46,821
Specialty Trade Contractors	$44,823
Machinery Manufacturing	$42,550
Professional, Scientific, and Technical Services	$41,288
Fabricated Metal Product Manufacturing	$40,342

DRYWALL INSTALLERS, CEILING TILE INSTALLERS, AND TAPERS

- Average Earnings: $35,936
- Beginning Earnings: $22,027
- 25th Percentile: $27,831
- 75th Percentile: $47,264

Average Earnings in Major Metropolitan Areas

Metropolitan Area	Average Annual Earnings
Atlanta, GA	$33,055
Chicago, IL	$49,060
Dallas-Fort Worth, TX	$27,660
Denver, CO	$31,376
Los Angeles, CA	$41,549
Minneapolis-St. Paul, MN	$57,174
New York, NY	$60,463
Phoenix, AZ	$28,870
San Francisco, CA	$60,193
Seattle, WA	$52,312

Average Earnings in Most Important Industries

Industry	Average Annual Earnings
Specialty Trade Contractors	$35,924

ECONOMISTS

- Average Earnings: $73,690
- Beginning Earnings: $40,810
- 25th Percentile: $53,100
- 75th Percentile: $99,920

Average Earnings in Major Metropolitan Areas

Metropolitan Area	Average Annual Earnings
Atlanta, GA	$79,570
Chicago, IL	$78,100
Denver, CO	$80,890
Los Angeles, CA	$78,650
Minneapolis-St. Paul, MN	$45,760
New York, NY	$87,540
Phoenix, AZ	$55,690
San Francisco, CA	$79,340

Average Earnings in Most Important Industries

Industry	Average Annual Earnings
Professional, Scientific, and Technical Services	$82,490
Management of Companies and Enterprises	$77,190
Educational Services	$50,340
Religious, Grantmaking, Civic, Professional, and Similar Organizations	$73,380
Federal, State, and Local Government	$71,270

EDUCATION ADMINISTRATORS

- Average Earnings: $68,650
- Beginning Earnings: $42,757
- 25th Percentile: $53,861
- 75th Percentile: $87,302

Average Earnings in Major Metropolitan Areas

Metropolitan Area	Average Annual Earnings
Atlanta, GA	$73,293
Chicago, IL	$76,420
Dallas-Fort Worth, TX	$60,707
Denver, CO	$68,642
Los Angeles, CA	$76,012
Minneapolis-St. Paul, MN	$77,464
New York, NY	$75,087
Phoenix, AZ	$70,072
San Francisco, CA	$80,089
Seattle, WA	$76,940

Average Earnings in Most Important Industries

Industry	Average Annual Earnings
Educational Services	$72,518
Hospitals	$71,133
Federal, State, and Local Government	$68,044
Religious, Grantmaking, Civic, Professional, and Similar Organizations	$45,266
Social Assistance	$35,409

ELECTRICAL AND ELECTRONICS INSTALLERS AND REPAIRERS

- Average Earnings: $41,895
- Beginning Earnings: $26,686
- 25th Percentile: $33,453
- 75th Percentile: $51,291

Average Earnings in Major Metropolitan Areas

Metropolitan Area	Average Annual Earnings
Atlanta, GA	$46,772
Chicago, IL	$46,814
Dallas-Fort Worth, TX	$40,455
Denver, CO	$42,453
Los Angeles, CA	$38,053
Minneapolis-St. Paul, MN	$34,931
New York, NY	$44,335
Phoenix, AZ	$47,124
San Francisco, CA	$40,764
Seattle, WA	$48,952

Average Earnings in Most Important Industries

Industry	Average Annual Earnings
Utilities	$55,714
Federal, State, and Local Government	$50,188
Transportation Equipment Manufacturing	$42,426
Merchant Wholesalers, Durable Goods	$36,895
Repair and Maintenance	$34,808

ELECTRICIANS

- Average Earnings: $42,790
- Beginning Earnings: $25,870
- 25th Percentile: $32,740
- 75th Percentile: $56,380

Average Earnings in Major Metropolitan Areas

Metropolitan Area	Average Annual Earnings
Atlanta, GA	$38,430
Chicago, IL	$57,440
Dallas-Fort Worth, TX	$36,430
Denver, CO	$44,830
Los Angeles, CA	$43,870
Minneapolis-St. Paul, MN	$64,590
New York, NY	$57,320
Phoenix, AZ	$36,030
San Francisco, CA	$64,170
Seattle, WA	$52,240

Average Earnings in Most Important Industries

Industry	Average Annual Earnings
Specialty Trade Contractors	$41,630

ELECTRONIC HOME ENTERTAINMENT EQUIPMENT INSTALLERS AND REPAIRERS

- Average Earnings: $28,940
- Beginning Earnings: $18,610
- 25th Percentile: $23,260
- 75th Percentile: $36,600

Average Earnings in Major Metropolitan Areas

Metropolitan Area	Average Annual Earnings
Atlanta, GA	$32,090
Chicago, IL	$36,210
Dallas-Fort Worth, TX	$27,560
Denver, CO	$36,880
Los Angeles, CA	$35,050
Minneapolis-St. Paul, MN	$33,700
New York, NY	$30,150
Phoenix, AZ	$20,890
San Francisco, CA	$34,710

Average Earnings in Most Important Industries

Industry	Average Annual Earnings
Broadcasting (Except Internet)	$32,710
Specialty Trade Contractors	$30,000
Telecommunications	$29,260
Electronics and Appliance Stores	$28,520
Rental and Leasing Services	$28,400

ELEVATOR INSTALLERS AND REPAIRERS

- Average Earnings: $59,190
- Beginning Earnings: $35,070
- 25th Percentile: $47,340
- 75th Percentile: $70,270

Average Earnings in Major Metropolitan Areas

Metropolitan Area	Average Annual Earnings
Atlanta, GA	$57,930
Chicago, IL	$72,230
Denver, CO	$55,480
Los Angeles, CA	$66,240
Minneapolis-St. Paul, MN	$48,750
Phoenix, AZ	$57,960
San Francisco, CA	$78,300
Seattle, WA	$74,870

Average Earnings in Most Important Industries

Industry	Average Annual Earnings
Specialty Trade Contractors	$59,880

EMERGENCY MEDICAL TECHNICIANS AND PARAMEDICS

- Average Earnings: $26,080
- Beginning Earnings: $16,620
- 25th Percentile: $20,470
- 75th Percentile: $34,310

Average Earnings in Major Metropolitan Areas

Metropolitan Area	Average Annual Earnings
Atlanta, GA	$32,500
Chicago, IL	$27,230
Dallas-Fort Worth, TX	$26,400
Denver, CO	$36,340
Los Angeles, CA	$21,960
Minneapolis-St. Paul, MN	$35,290
New York, NY	$37,740
Phoenix, AZ	$22,250
Seattle, WA	$34,760

Average Earnings in Most Important Industries

Industry	Average Annual Earnings
Federal, State, and Local Government	$27,890
Hospitals	$27,420
Ambulatory Health Care Services	$24,390

ENGINEERING AND NATURAL SCIENCES MANAGERS

- Average Earnings: $99,400
- Beginning Earnings: $62,509
- 25th Percentile: $78,403
- 75th Percentile: $124,292

Average Earnings in Major Metropolitan Areas

Metropolitan Area	Average Annual Earnings
Atlanta, GA	$86,979
Chicago, IL	$89,077
Dallas-Fort Worth, TX	$105,076
Denver, CO	$101,803
Los Angeles, CA	$108,102
Minneapolis-St. Paul, MN	$102,940
New York, NY	$120,428
Phoenix, AZ	$98,710
San Francisco, CA	$120,694
Seattle, WA	$115,940

Average Earnings in Most Important Industries

Industry	Average Annual Earnings
Computer and Electronic Product Manufacturing	$115,537
Professional, Scientific, and Technical Services	$104,967
Transportation Equipment Manufacturing	$100,451
Machinery Manufacturing	$90,616
Federal, State, and Local Government	$87,579

ENGINEERING TECHNICIANS

- Average Earnings: $46,075
- Beginning Earnings: $28,700
- 25th Percentile: $36,355
- 75th Percentile: $56,731

Average Earnings in Major Metropolitan Areas

Metropolitan Area	Average Annual Earnings
Atlanta, GA	$42,019
Chicago, IL	$41,219
Dallas-Fort Worth, TX	$47,817
Denver, CO	$47,461
Los Angeles, CA	$48,227
Minneapolis-St. Paul, MN	$48,534
New York, NY	$51,582
Phoenix, AZ	$42,341
San Francisco, CA	$53,978
Seattle, WA	$55,334

Average Earnings in Most Important Industries

Industry	Average Annual Earnings
Transportation Equipment Manufacturing	$49,644
Federal, State, and Local Government	$47,612
Machinery Manufacturing	$44,531
Computer and Electronic Product Manufacturing	$44,282
Professional, Scientific, and Technical Services	$43,919

ENGINEERS

- Average Earnings: $72,466
- Beginning Earnings: $46,436
- 25th Percentile: $57,507
- 75th Percentile: $89,904

Average Earnings in Major Metropolitan Areas

Metropolitan Area	Average Annual Earnings
Atlanta, GA	$67,116
Chicago, IL	$67,867
Dallas-Fort Worth, TX	$76,171
Denver, CO	$72,181
Los Angeles, CA	$77,315
Minneapolis-St. Paul, MN	$70,656
New York, NY	$77,104
Phoenix, AZ	$71,061
San Francisco, CA	$82,064
Seattle, WA	$70,986

Average Earnings in Most Important Industries

Industry	Average Annual Earnings
Computer and Electronic Product Manufacturing	$79,089
Federal, State, and Local Government	$75,463
Professional, Scientific, and Technical Services	$73,041
Transportation Equipment Manufacturing	$72,420
Machinery Manufacturing	$63,576

ENVIRONMENTAL SCIENTISTS AND HYDROLOGISTS

- Average Earnings: $53,794
- Beginning Earnings: $33,667
- 25th Percentile: $41,439
- 75th Percentile: $71,042

Average Earnings in Major Metropolitan Areas

Metropolitan Area	Average Annual Earnings
Atlanta, GA	$53,317
Chicago, IL	$53,280
Dallas-Fort Worth, TX	$57,491
Denver, CO	$73,577
Los Angeles, CA	$65,357
Minneapolis-St. Paul, MN	$54,510
New York, NY	$58,938
Phoenix, AZ	$45,450
San Francisco, CA	$72,673
Seattle, WA	$61,134

Average Earnings in Most Important Industries

Industry	Average Annual Earnings
Professional, Scientific, and Technical Services	$55,390
Waste Management and Remediation Services	$53,050
Federal, State, and Local Government	$53,004
Religious, Grantmaking, Civic, Professional, and Similar Organizations	$48,952
Educational Services	$42,550

FARMERS, RANCHERS, AND AGRICULTURAL MANAGERS

- Average Earnings: $49,812
- Beginning Earnings: $29,711
- 25th Percentile: $38,750
- 75th Percentile: $64,628

Average Earnings in Major Metropolitan Areas

Metropolitan Area	Average Annual Earnings
New York, NY	$76,240

Average Earnings in Most Important Industries

Industry	Average Annual Earnings
Merchant Wholesalers, Nondurable Goods	$54,690
Administrative and Support Services	$54,540
Educational Services	$52,690
Support Activities for Agriculture and Forestry	$47,738
Building Material and Garden Equipment and Supplies Dealers	$39,720

FASHION DESIGNERS

- Average Earnings: $60,860
- Beginning Earnings: $30,600
- 25th Percentile: $41,140
- 75th Percentile: $87,300

Average Earnings in Major Metropolitan Areas

Metropolitan Area	Average Annual Earnings
Chicago, IL	$50,680
Dallas-Fort Worth, TX	$43,840
Los Angeles, CA	$53,670
Minneapolis-St. Paul, MN	$47,570
New York, NY	$68,990
Seattle, WA	$61,360

Average Earnings in Most Important Industries

Industry	Average Annual Earnings
Apparel Manufacturing	$68,840
Professional, Scientific, and Technical Services	$66,870
Management of Companies and Enterprises	$66,420
Clothing and Clothing Accessories Stores	$62,210
Merchant Wholesalers, Nondurable Goods	$58,590

FILE CLERKS

- Average Earnings: $21,430
- Beginning Earnings: $14,690
- 25th Percentile: $17,460
- 75th Percentile: $26,830

Average Earnings in Major Metropolitan Areas

Metropolitan Area	Average Annual Earnings
Atlanta, GA	$21,460
Chicago, IL	$22,470
Dallas-Fort Worth, TX	$23,920
Denver, CO	$25,410
Los Angeles, CA	$22,260
Minneapolis-St. Paul, MN	$24,650
New York, NY	$24,030
Phoenix, AZ	$20,950
San Francisco, CA	$27,000
Seattle, WA	$25,280

Average Earnings in Most Important Industries

Industry	Average Annual Earnings
Federal, State, and Local Government	$25,620
Hospitals	$21,990
Professional, Scientific, and Technical Services	$21,940
Administrative and Support Services	$21,060
Ambulatory Health Care Services	$19,480

FINANCIAL ANALYSTS AND PERSONAL FINANCIAL ADVISORS

- Average Earnings: $63,725
- Beginning Earnings: $35,708
- 25th Percentile: $46,146
- 75th Percentile: $94,480

Average Earnings in Major Metropolitan Areas

Metropolitan Area	Average Annual Earnings
Atlanta, GA	$61,736
Chicago, IL	$62,273
Dallas-Fort Worth, TX	$63,060
Denver, CO	$61,347
Los Angeles, CA	$67,430
Minneapolis-St. Paul, MN	$60,244
New York, NY	$82,423
Phoenix, AZ	$55,710
San Francisco, CA	$77,828
Seattle, WA	$66,857

Average Earnings in Most Important Industries

Industry	Average Annual Earnings
Securities, Commodity Contracts, and Other Financial Investments and Related Activities	$73,100
Management of Companies and Enterprises	$63,448
Professional, Scientific, and Technical Services	$60,943
Insurance Carriers and Related Activities	$56,820
Credit Intermediation and Related Activities	$57,319

FINANCIAL MANAGERS

- Average Earnings: $86,280
- Beginning Earnings: $47,910
- 25th Percentile: $63,160
- 75th Percentile: $118,150

Average Earnings in Major Metropolitan Areas

Metropolitan Area	Average Annual Earnings
Atlanta, GA	$85,190
Chicago, IL	$89,930
Dallas-Fort Worth, TX	$86,940
Denver, CO	$91,440
Los Angeles, CA	$94,200
Minneapolis-St. Paul, MN	$98,910
New York, NY	$125,200
Phoenix, AZ	$78,930
San Francisco, CA	$103,360
Seattle, WA	$95,360

Average Earnings in Most Important Industries

Industry	Average Annual Earnings
Securities, Commodity Contracts, and Other Financial Investments and Related Activities	$132,390
Management of Companies and Enterprises	$99,280
Professional, Scientific, and Technical Services	$97,280
Federal, State, and Local Government	$76,680
Credit Intermediation and Related Activities	$73,960

FIRE FIGHTING OCCUPATIONS

- Average Earnings: $42,681
- Beginning Earnings: $22,685
- 25th Percentile: $31,667
- 75th Percentile: $55,400

Average Earnings in Major Metropolitan Areas

Metropolitan Area	Average Annual Earnings
Atlanta, GA	$39,481
Chicago, IL	$52,428
Dallas-Fort Worth, TX	$45,728
Denver, CO	$54,354
Los Angeles, CA	$63,491
Minneapolis-St. Paul, MN	$27,979
New York, NY	$40,500
Phoenix, AZ	$50,833
San Francisco, CA	$99,244
Seattle, WA	$57,687

Average Earnings in Most Important Industries

Industry	Average Annual Earnings
Federal, State, and Local Government	$42,954

FISHERS AND FISHING VESSEL OPERATORS

- Average Earnings: $25,130
- Beginning Earnings: $15,290
- 25th Percentile: $18,420
- 75th Percentile: $37,230

Average Earnings in Major Metropolitan Areas

Metropolitan Area	Average Annual Earnings
New York, NY	$19,950

Average Earnings in Most Important Industries

Industry	Average Annual Earnings
Federal, State, and Local Government	$32,920
Food Manufacturing	$22,390
Scenic and Sightseeing Transportation	$18,780

FITNESS WORKERS

- Average Earnings: $25,840
- Beginning Earnings: $14,540
- 25th Percentile: $17,600
- 75th Percentile: $40,260

Average Earnings in Major Metropolitan Areas

Metropolitan Area	Average Annual Earnings
Atlanta, GA	$27,250
Chicago, IL	$29,780
Dallas-Fort Worth, TX	$32,000
Denver, CO	$32,310
Los Angeles, CA	$35,380
Minneapolis-St. Paul, MN	$23,820
New York, NY	$39,210
Phoenix, AZ	$24,840
San Francisco, CA	$47,370

Average Earnings in Most Important Industries

Industry	Average Annual Earnings
Hospitals	$29,210
Amusement, Gambling, and Recreation Industries	$27,830
Federal, State, and Local Government	$25,060
Religious, Grantmaking, Civic, Professional, and Similar Organizations	$22,000
Educational Services	$21,860

FLIGHT ATTENDANTS

- Average Earnings: $46,680
- Beginning Earnings: $25,940
- 25th Percentile: $32,420
- 75th Percentile: $71,190

Average Earnings in Major Metropolitan Areas

Metropolitan Area	Average Annual Earnings
Chicago, IL	$34,980
New York, NY	$63,610

Average Earnings in Most Important Industries

Industry	Average Annual Earnings
Air Transportation	$46,640

FLORAL DESIGNERS

- Average Earnings: $21,060
- Beginning Earnings: $14,710
- 25th Percentile: $17,250
- 75th Percentile: $26,360

Average Earnings in Major Metropolitan Areas

Metropolitan Area	Average Annual Earnings
Atlanta, GA	$23,750
Chicago, IL	$22,680
Dallas-Fort Worth, TX	$21,720
Denver, CO	$22,880
Los Angeles, CA	$25,140
Minneapolis-St. Paul, MN	$23,550
New York, NY	$26,590
Phoenix, AZ	$21,800
San Francisco, CA	$28,750
Seattle, WA	$27,210

Average Earnings in Most Important Industries

Industry	Average Annual Earnings
Food and Beverage Stores	$22,580
Building Material and Garden Equipment and Supplies Dealers	$22,000
Miscellaneous Store Retailers	$20,720
Sporting Goods, Hobby, Book, and Music Stores	$20,650
Merchant Wholesalers, Nondurable Goods	$19,540

FOOD AND BEVERAGE SERVING AND RELATED WORKERS

- Average Earnings: $14,945
- Beginning Earnings: $11,938
- 25th Percentile: $13,198
- 75th Percentile: $17,864

Average Earnings in Major Metropolitan Areas

Metropolitan Area	Average Annual Earnings
Atlanta, GA	$13,983
Chicago, IL	$14,776
Dallas-Fort Worth, TX	$13,746
Denver, CO	$15,717
Los Angeles, CA	$16,588
Minneapolis-St. Paul, MN	$15,764
New York, NY	$17,712
Phoenix, AZ	$14,327
San Francisco, CA	$17,685
Seattle, WA	$17,793

Average Earnings in Most Important Industries

Industry	Average Annual Earnings
Food Services and Drinking Places	$14,586

FOOD PROCESSING OCCUPATIONS

- Average Earnings: $22,236
- Beginning Earnings: $15,113
- 25th Percentile: $17,877
- 75th Percentile: $27,811

Average Earnings in Major Metropolitan Areas

Metropolitan Area	Average Annual Earnings
Atlanta, GA	$21,291
Chicago, IL	$23,115
Dallas-Fort Worth, TX	$21,373
Denver, CO	$29,324
Los Angeles, CA	$20,603
Minneapolis-St. Paul, MN	$30,656
New York, NY	$25,279
Phoenix, AZ	$24,184
San Francisco, CA	$27,686
Seattle, WA	$28,199

Average Earnings in Most Important Industries

Industry	Average Annual Earnings
General Merchandise Stores	$27,103
Food and Beverage Stores	$23,861
Merchant Wholesalers, Nondurable Goods	$22,110
Food Manufacturing	$21,655
Food Services and Drinking Places	$19,980

FOOD SERVICE MANAGERS

- Average Earnings: $41,340
- Beginning Earnings: $25,990
- 25th Percentile: $32,690
- 75th Percentile: $52,810

Average Earnings in Major Metropolitan Areas

Metropolitan Area	Average Annual Earnings
Atlanta, GA	$44,520
Chicago, IL	$40,990
Dallas-Fort Worth, TX	$50,620
Denver, CO	$49,730
Los Angeles, CA	$42,730
Minneapolis-St. Paul, MN	$40,360
New York, NY	$51,650
Phoenix, AZ	$39,350
San Francisco, CA	$43,610
Seattle, WA	$75,620

Average Earnings in Most Important Industries

Industry	Average Annual Earnings
Food Services and Drinking Places	$40,760

FOREST, CONSERVATION, AND LOGGING WORKERS

- Average Earnings: $27,086
- Beginning Earnings: $17,890
- 25th Percentile: $21,677
- 75th Percentile: $34,072

Average Earnings in Major Metropolitan Areas

Metropolitan Area	Average Annual Earnings
Atlanta, GA	$33,960
Chicago, IL	$30,570
Los Angeles, CA	$51,890
New York, NY	$16,730
Seattle, WA	$36,064

Average Earnings in Most Important Industries

Industry	Average Annual Earnings
Forestry and Logging	$29,597
Wood Product Manufacturing	$26,493
Federal, State, and Local Government	$19,056

FUNERAL DIRECTORS

- Average Earnings: $47,630
- Beginning Earnings: $27,670
- 25th Percentile: $36,540
- 75th Percentile: $63,010

Average Earnings in Major Metropolitan Areas

Metropolitan Area	Average Annual Earnings
Atlanta, GA	$44,110
Chicago, IL	$60,970
Dallas-Fort Worth, TX	$36,450
Denver, CO	$40,810
Los Angeles, CA	$44,150
Minneapolis-St. Paul, MN	$52,740
New York, NY	$59,690
Phoenix, AZ	$47,470
San Francisco, CA	$42,140

Average Earnings in Most Important Industries

Industry	Average Annual Earnings
Personal and Laundry Services	$47,620

GAMING CAGE WORKERS

- Average Earnings: $22,380
- Beginning Earnings: $16,720
- 25th Percentile: $19,360
- 75th Percentile: $27,130

Average Earnings in Major Metropolitan Areas

Metropolitan Area	Average Annual Earnings
Denver, CO	$28,370
San Francisco, CA	$24,970

Average Earnings in Most Important Industries

Industry	Average Annual Earnings
Accommodation	$24,120
Performing Arts, Spectator Sports, and Related Industries	$24,030
Amusement, Gambling, and Recreation Industries	$21,840
Federal, State, and Local Government	$21,570

GAMING SERVICES OCCUPATIONS

- Average Earnings: $20,138
- Beginning Earnings: $14,563
- 25th Percentile: $17,015
- 75th Percentile: $24,437

Average Earnings in Major Metropolitan Areas

Metropolitan Area	Average Annual Earnings
Chicago, IL	$23,070
Dallas-Fort Worth, TX	$15,410
Denver, CO	$22,430
Los Angeles, CA	$17,207
Minneapolis-St. Paul, MN	$18,340
New York, NY	$45,046
Phoenix, AZ	$20,810
San Francisco, CA	$22,444
Seattle, WA	$20,387

Average Earnings in Most Important Industries

Industry	Average Annual Earnings
Accommodation	$20,973
Federal, State, and Local Government	$20,823
Performing Arts, Spectator Sports, and Related Industries	$18,650
Amusement, Gambling, and Recreation Industries	$19,341
Religious, Grantmaking, Civic, Professional, and Similar Organizations	$15,717

GEOSCIENTISTS

- Average Earnings: $58,335
- Beginning Earnings: $35,131
- 25th Percentile: $44,144
- 75th Percentile: $78,892

Average Earnings in Major Metropolitan Areas

Metropolitan Area	Average Annual Earnings
Atlanta, GA	$53,270
Chicago, IL	$55,533
Dallas-Fort Worth, TX	$65,156
Denver, CO	$80,322
Los Angeles, CA	$65,541
Minneapolis-St. Paul, MN	$55,613
New York, NY	$60,328
Phoenix, AZ	$47,119
San Francisco, CA	$74,869
Seattle, WA	$63,825

Average Earnings in Most Important Industries

Industry	Average Annual Earnings
Oil and Gas Extraction	$101,584
Support Activities for Mining	$94,550
Professional, Scientific, and Technical Services	$57,830
Federal, State, and Local Government	$54,544
Educational Services	$45,254

GLAZIERS

- Average Earnings: $33,530
- Beginning Earnings: $20,640
- 25th Percentile: $26,060
- 75th Percentile: $44,470

Average Earnings in Major Metropolitan Areas

Metropolitan Area	Average Annual Earnings
Atlanta, GA	$31,220
Chicago, IL	$62,160
Dallas-Fort Worth, TX	$30,690
Denver, CO	$38,810
Los Angeles, CA	$31,640
Minneapolis-St. Paul, MN	$36,980
New York, NY	$39,590
San Francisco, CA	$64,120
Seattle, WA	$41,810

Average Earnings in Most Important Industries

Industry	Average Annual Earnings
Specialty Trade Contractors	$34,140

GRAPHIC DESIGNERS

- Average Earnings: $38,390
- Beginning Earnings: $23,160
- 25th Percentile: $29,460
- 75th Percentile: $51,360

Average Earnings in Major Metropolitan Areas

Metropolitan Area	Average Annual Earnings
Atlanta, GA	$43,140
Chicago, IL	$39,610
Dallas-Fort Worth, TX	$39,320
Denver, CO	$36,230
Los Angeles, CA	$42,150
Minneapolis-St. Paul, MN	$42,250
New York, NY	$50,120
Phoenix, AZ	$36,540
San Francisco, CA	$53,890
Seattle, WA	$45,970

Average Earnings in Most Important Industries

Industry	Average Annual Earnings
Professional, Scientific, and Technical Services	$41,750
Educational Services	$38,030
Publishing Industries (Except Internet)	$33,520
Printing and Related Support Activities	$33,500
Miscellaneous Manufacturing	$31,950

GROUNDS MAINTENANCE WORKERS

- Average Earnings: $22,550
- Beginning Earnings: $15,740
- 25th Percentile: $18,304
- 75th Percentile: $28,552

Average Earnings in Major Metropolitan Areas

Metropolitan Area	Average Annual Earnings
Atlanta, GA	$23,249
Chicago, IL	$22,737
Dallas-Fort Worth, TX	$21,276
Denver, CO	$24,189
Los Angeles, CA	$22,642
Minneapolis-St. Paul, MN	$27,299
New York, NY	$26,568
Phoenix, AZ	$19,788
San Francisco, CA	$28,252
Seattle, WA	$26,973

Average Earnings in Most Important Industries

Industry	Average Annual Earnings
Educational Services	$26,290
Federal, State, and Local Government	$26,282
Administrative and Support Services	$22,165
Real Estate	$21,297
Amusement, Gambling, and Recreation Industries	$21,441

HAZARDOUS MATERIALS REMOVAL WORKERS

- Average Earnings: $33,690
- Beginning Earnings: $21,470
- 25th Percentile: $26,210
- 75th Percentile: $46,960

Average Earnings in Major Metropolitan Areas

Metropolitan Area	Average Annual Earnings
Atlanta, GA	$26,490
Chicago, IL	$41,390
Dallas-Fort Worth, TX	$24,920
Denver, CO	$33,150
Los Angeles, CA	$29,960
Minneapolis-St. Paul, MN	$50,990
New York, NY	$49,590
Phoenix, AZ	$27,050
San Francisco, CA	$33,460
Seattle, WA	$46,540

Average Earnings in Most Important Industries

Industry	Average Annual Earnings
Waste Management and Remediation Services	$33,240

HEATING, AIR-CONDITIONING, AND REFRIGERATION MECHANICS AND INSTALLERS

- Average Earnings: $37,040
- Beginning Earnings: $22,970
- 25th Percentile: $28,690
- 75th Percentile: $47,270

Average Earnings in Major Metropolitan Areas

Metropolitan Area	Average Annual Earnings
Atlanta, GA	$40,950
Chicago, IL	$42,620
Dallas-Fort Worth, TX	$35,350
Denver, CO	$46,400
Los Angeles, CA	$46,460
Minneapolis-St. Paul, MN	$44,450
New York, NY	$47,870
Phoenix, AZ	$37,710
San Francisco, CA	$47,800
Seattle, WA	$49,510

Average Earnings in Most Important Industries

Industry	Average Annual Earnings
Specialty Trade Contractors	$35,560

HEAVY VEHICLE AND MOBILE EQUIPMENT SERVICE TECHNICIANS AND MECHANICS

- Average Earnings: $37,943
- Beginning Earnings: $24,662
- 25th Percentile: $30,894
- 75th Percentile: $45,296

Average Earnings in Major Metropolitan Areas

Metropolitan Area	Average Annual Earnings
Atlanta, GA	$40,019
Chicago, IL	$44,463
Dallas-Fort Worth, TX	$33,837
Denver, CO	$41,420
Los Angeles, CA	$49,299
Minneapolis-St. Paul, MN	$45,594
New York, NY	$49,340
Phoenix, AZ	$37,398
San Francisco, CA	$57,800
Seattle, WA	$49,236

Average Earnings in Most Important Industries

Industry	Average Annual Earnings
Rail Transportation	$43,284
Federal, State, and Local Government	$41,938
Heavy and Civil Engineering Construction	$38,347
Specialty Trade Contractors	$36,930
Merchant Wholesalers, Durable Goods	$35,049

HOME APPLIANCE REPAIRERS

- Average Earnings: $32,980
- Beginning Earnings: $18,840
- 25th Percentile: $24,850
- 75th Percentile: $41,850

Average Earnings in Major Metropolitan Areas

Metropolitan Area	Average Annual Earnings
Atlanta, GA	$29,850
Chicago, IL	$38,910
Dallas-Fort Worth, TX	$31,820
Denver, CO	$39,040
Los Angeles, CA	$32,760
Minneapolis-St. Paul, MN	$39,570
New York, NY	$39,080
Phoenix, AZ	$36,440
San Francisco, CA	$43,750
Seattle, WA	$42,270

Average Earnings in Most Important Industries

Industry	Average Annual Earnings
Utilities	$54,010
Warehousing and Storage	$37,380
Repair and Maintenance	$34,290
Electronics and Appliance Stores	$31,580
Merchant Wholesalers, Durable Goods	$30,010

HOTEL, MOTEL, AND RESORT DESK CLERKS

- Average Earnings: $17,810
- Beginning Earnings: $13,320
- 25th Percentile: $15,360
- 75th Percentile: $21,490

Average Earnings in Major Metropolitan Areas

Metropolitan Area	Average Annual Earnings
Atlanta, GA	$17,330
Chicago, IL	$19,690
Dallas-Fort Worth, TX	$18,750
Denver, CO	$19,770
Los Angeles, CA	$20,290
Minneapolis-St. Paul, MN	$20,650
New York, NY	$22,460
Phoenix, AZ	$19,410
San Francisco, CA	$26,290
Seattle, WA	$20,440

Average Earnings in Most Important Industries

Industry	Average Annual Earnings
Accommodation	$17,720

HUMAN RESOURCES ASSISTANTS, EXCEPT PAYROLL AND TIMEKEEPING

- Average Earnings: $32,730
- Beginning Earnings: $22,080
- 25th Percentile: $26,580
- 75th Percentile: $40,100

Average Earnings in Major Metropolitan Areas

Metropolitan Area	Average Annual Earnings
Chicago, IL	$32,500
Dallas-Fort Worth, TX	$33,520
Denver, CO	$37,230
Los Angeles, CA	$37,040
Minneapolis-St. Paul, MN	$35,390
New York, NY	$36,270
Phoenix, AZ	$32,800
San Francisco, CA	$41,930
Seattle, WA	$36,550

Average Earnings in Most Important Industries

Industry	Average Annual Earnings
Federal, State, and Local Government	$35,900
Professional, Scientific, and Technical Services	$35,820
Management of Companies and Enterprises	$33,150
Educational Services	$32,830
Administrative and Support Services	$29,080

HUMAN RESOURCES, TRAINING, AND LABOR RELATIONS MANAGERS AND SPECIALISTS

- Average Earnings: $51,173
- Beginning Earnings: $27,962
- 25th Percentile: $38,669
- 75th Percentile: $67,257

Average Earnings in Major Metropolitan Areas

Metropolitan Area	Average Annual Earnings
Atlanta, GA	$54,624
Chicago, IL	$49,935
Dallas-Fort Worth, TX	$53,333
Denver, CO	$54,541
Los Angeles, CA	$59,484
Minneapolis-St. Paul, MN	$57,721
New York, NY	$61,505
Phoenix, AZ	$45,023
San Francisco, CA	$66,849
Seattle, WA	$59,154

Average Earnings in Most Important Industries

Industry	Average Annual Earnings
Management of Companies and Enterprises	$61,922
Professional, Scientific, and Technical Services	$58,907
Federal, State, and Local Government	$49,642
Religious, Grantmaking, Civic, Professional, and Similar Organizations	$42,684
Administrative and Support Services	$41,854

INDUSTRIAL MACHINERY MECHANICS AND MAINTENANCE WORKERS

- Average Earnings: $38,146
- Beginning Earnings: $24,636
- 25th Percentile: $30,461
- 75th Percentile: $47,479

Average Earnings in Major Metropolitan Areas

Metropolitan Area	Average Annual Earnings
Atlanta, GA	$35,837
Chicago, IL	$42,367
Dallas-Fort Worth, TX	$38,353
Denver, CO	$44,880
Los Angeles, CA	$38,174
Minneapolis-St. Paul, MN	$42,990
New York, NY	$42,463
Phoenix, AZ	$43,050
San Francisco, CA	$48,041
Seattle, WA	$48,120

Average Earnings in Most Important Industries

Industry	Average Annual Earnings
Transportation Equipment Manufacturing	$46,306
Chemical Manufacturing	$43,235
Merchant Wholesalers, Durable Goods	$36,090
Food Manufacturing	$35,575
Repair and Maintenance	$34,905

INDUSTRIAL PRODUCTION MANAGERS

- Average Earnings: $75,580
- Beginning Earnings: $46,300
- 25th Percentile: $58,260
- 75th Percentile: $97,830

Average Earnings in Major Metropolitan Areas

Metropolitan Area	Average Annual Earnings
Atlanta, GA	$73,700
Chicago, IL	$72,560
Dallas-Fort Worth, TX	$85,050
Denver, CO	$67,460
Los Angeles, CA	$75,180
Minneapolis-St. Paul, MN	$81,170
New York, NY	$90,100
Phoenix, AZ	$78,390
San Francisco, CA	$86,930
Seattle, WA	$83,700

Average Earnings in Most Important Industries

Industry	Average Annual Earnings
Computer and Electronic Product Manufacturing	$87,470
Chemical Manufacturing	$82,750
Transportation Equipment Manufacturing	$79,700
Machinery Manufacturing	$75,600
Fabricated Metal Product Manufacturing	$69,480

INSPECTORS, TESTERS, SORTERS, SAMPLERS, AND WEIGHERS

- Average Earnings: $29,200
- Beginning Earnings: $17,790
- 25th Percentile: $22,300
- 75th Percentile: $39,690

Average Earnings in Major Metropolitan Areas

Metropolitan Area	Average Annual Earnings
Atlanta, GA	$28,530
Chicago, IL	$27,880
Dallas-Fort Worth, TX	$27,770
Denver, CO	$32,190
Los Angeles, CA	$25,200
Minneapolis-St. Paul, MN	$33,370
New York, NY	$29,100
Phoenix, AZ	$26,810
San Francisco, CA	$32,800
Seattle, WA	$41,080

Average Earnings in Most Important Industries

Industry	Average Annual Earnings
Transportation Equipment Manufacturing	$38,480
Fabricated Metal Product Manufacturing	$30,580
Computer and Electronic Product Manufacturing	$29,480
Plastics and Rubber Products Manufacturing	$27,500
Administrative and Support Services	$23,650

INSTRUCTIONAL COORDINATORS

- Average Earnings: $50,430
- Beginning Earnings: $28,560
- 25th Percentile: $37,030
- 75th Percentile: $67,370

Average Earnings in Major Metropolitan Areas

Metropolitan Area	Average Annual Earnings
Atlanta, GA	$47,880
Chicago, IL	$51,670
Dallas-Fort Worth, TX	$60,930
Denver, CO	$61,710
Los Angeles, CA	$52,580
Minneapolis-St. Paul, MN	$60,440
New York, NY	$58,960
Phoenix, AZ	$39,220
San Francisco, CA	$48,040
Seattle, WA	$51,610

Average Earnings in Most Important Industries

Industry	Average Annual Earnings
Federal, State, and Local Government	$54,730
Professional, Scientific, and Technical Services	$54,610
Educational Services	$51,880
Social Assistance	$34,530
Museums, Historical Sites, and Similar Institutions	$32,700

INSULATION WORKERS

- Average Earnings: $32,988
- Beginning Earnings: $19,814
- 25th Percentile: $24,780
- 75th Percentile: $45,106

Average Earnings in Major Metropolitan Areas

Metropolitan Area	Average Annual Earnings
Atlanta, GA	$36,430
Chicago, IL	$64,010
Denver, CO	$29,580
Los Angeles, CA	$33,363
Minneapolis-St. Paul, MN	$50,284
New York, NY	$48,584
San Francisco, CA	$59,720

Average Earnings in Most Important Industries

Industry	Average Annual Earnings
Specialty Trade Contractors	$32,708

INSURANCE SALES AGENTS

- Average Earnings: $42,340
- Beginning Earnings: $23,630
- 25th Percentile: $30,330
- 75th Percentile: $68,050

Average Earnings in Major Metropolitan Areas

Metropolitan Area	Average Annual Earnings
Atlanta, GA	$47,320
Chicago, IL	$47,310
Dallas-Fort Worth, TX	$41,580
Denver, CO	$48,850
Los Angeles, CA	$53,230
Minneapolis-St. Paul, MN	$56,060
New York, NY	$52,290
Phoenix, AZ	$42,040
San Francisco, CA	$66,280
Seattle, WA	$53,970

Average Earnings in Most Important Industries

Industry	Average Annual Earnings
Insurance Carriers and Related Activities	$42,490

INSURANCE UNDERWRITERS

- Average Earnings: $51,270
- Beginning Earnings: $31,350
- 25th Percentile: $39,000
- 75th Percentile: $69,110

Average Earnings in Major Metropolitan Areas

Metropolitan Area	Average Annual Earnings
Atlanta, GA	$57,400
Chicago, IL	$50,100
Dallas-Fort Worth, TX	$52,340
Denver, CO	$55,660
Los Angeles, CA	$57,860
Minneapolis-St. Paul, MN	$53,810
New York, NY	$61,870
Phoenix, AZ	$43,770
San Francisco, CA	$60,470
Seattle, WA	$54,680

Average Earnings in Most Important Industries

Industry	Average Annual Earnings
Insurance Carriers and Related Activities	$51,630

INTERIOR DESIGNERS

- Average Earnings: $41,350
- Beginning Earnings: $23,820
- 25th Percentile: $31,080
- 75th Percentile: $55,540

Average Earnings in Major Metropolitan Areas

Metropolitan Area	Average Annual Earnings
Atlanta, GA	$46,290
Chicago, IL	$43,870
Dallas-Fort Worth, TX	$41,730
Denver, CO	$43,830
Los Angeles, CA	$43,820
Minneapolis-St. Paul, MN	$45,590
New York, NY	$51,300
Phoenix, AZ	$35,300
San Francisco, CA	$55,360
Seattle, WA	$43,350

Average Earnings in Most Important Industries

Industry	Average Annual Earnings
Management of Companies and Enterprises	$50,430
Professional, Scientific, and Technical Services	$44,240
Merchant Wholesalers, Durable Goods	$41,620
Furniture and Related Product Manufacturing	$40,280
Furniture and Home Furnishings Stores	$37,870

INTERPRETERS AND TRANSLATORS

- Average Earnings: $34,800
- Beginning Earnings: $20,540
- 25th Percentile: $26,970
- 75th Percentile: $45,920

Average Earnings in Major Metropolitan Areas

Metropolitan Area	Average Annual Earnings
Atlanta, GA	$34,460
Chicago, IL	$31,780
Dallas-Fort Worth, TX	$35,400
Denver, CO	$54,050
Los Angeles, CA	$36,390
Minneapolis-St. Paul, MN	$38,480
New York, NY	$36,090
Phoenix, AZ	$32,360
San Francisco, CA	$55,510
Seattle, WA	$43,440

Average Earnings in Most Important Industries

Industry	Average Annual Earnings
Federal, State, and Local Government	$38,330
Professional, Scientific, and Technical Services	$36,590
Hospitals	$34,750
Educational Services	$34,390
Social Assistance	$32,240

INTERVIEWERS

- Average Earnings: $28,805
- Beginning Earnings: $19,248
- 25th Percentile: $23,286
- 75th Percentile: $35,559

Average Earnings in Major Metropolitan Areas

Metropolitan Area	Average Annual Earnings
Atlanta, GA	$24,036
Chicago, IL	$27,557
Dallas-Fort Worth, TX	$26,928
Denver, CO	$32,589
Los Angeles, CA	$32,200
Minneapolis-St. Paul, MN	$32,431
New York, NY	$32,052
Phoenix, AZ	$27,091
San Francisco, CA	$36,130
Seattle, WA	$31,917

Average Earnings in Most Important Industries

Industry	Average Annual Earnings
Federal, State, and Local Government	$33,645
Credit Intermediation and Related Activities	$29,824
Hospitals	$25,701
Ambulatory Health Care Services	$25,609
Professional, Scientific, and Technical Services	$22,419

JEWELERS AND PRECIOUS STONE AND METAL WORKERS

- Average Earnings: $29,430
- Beginning Earnings: $17,590
- 25th Percentile: $22,200
- 75th Percentile: $40,030

Average Earnings in Major Metropolitan Areas

Metropolitan Area	Average Annual Earnings
Atlanta, GA	$36,440
Chicago, IL	$28,970
Dallas-Fort Worth, TX	$35,280
Denver, CO	$28,330
Los Angeles, CA	$24,990
Minneapolis-St. Paul, MN	$41,330
New York, NY	$31,840
San Francisco, CA	$34,880
Seattle, WA	$36,680

Average Earnings in Most Important Industries

Industry	Average Annual Earnings
Merchant Wholesalers, Durable Goods	$33,190
Clothing and Clothing Accessories Stores	$31,700
Repair and Maintenance	$28,520
Professional, Scientific, and Technical Services	$29,370
Miscellaneous Manufacturing	$25,450

JUDGES, MAGISTRATES, AND OTHER JUDICIAL WORKERS

- Average Earnings: $83,310
- Beginning Earnings: $29,618
- 25th Percentile: $48,379
- 75th Percentile: $110,917

Average Earnings in Major Metropolitan Areas

Metropolitan Area	Average Annual Earnings
Atlanta, GA	$77,317
Chicago, IL	$125,380
Dallas-Fort Worth, TX	$73,935
Denver, CO	$84,507
Los Angeles, CA	$93,663
Minneapolis-St. Paul, MN	$74,654
New York, NY	$116,447
Phoenix, AZ	$66,131
San Francisco, CA	$107,914

Average Earnings in Most Important Industries

Industry	Average Annual Earnings
Federal, State, and Local Government	$85,650

LANDSCAPE ARCHITECTS

- Average Earnings: $54,220
- Beginning Earnings: $33,570
- 25th Percentile: $42,150
- 75th Percentile: $71,220

Average Earnings in Major Metropolitan Areas

Metropolitan Area	Average Annual Earnings
Chicago, IL	$52,330
Dallas-Fort Worth, TX	$54,120
Denver, CO	$51,750
Los Angeles, CA	$64,520
Minneapolis-St. Paul, MN	$52,330
New York, NY	$60,180
Phoenix, AZ	$49,400
San Francisco, CA	$64,310

Average Earnings in Most Important Industries

Industry	Average Annual Earnings
Federal, State, and Local Government	$63,800
Professional, Scientific, and Technical Services	$54,130
Administrative and Support Services	$50,080
Heavy and Civil Engineering Construction	$48,370
Building Material and Garden Equipment and Supplies Dealers	$44,040

LAWYERS

- Average Earnings: $98,930
- Beginning Earnings: $49,180
- 25th Percentile: $67,540
- 75th Percentile: more than $146,000

Average Earnings in Major Metropolitan Areas

Metropolitan Area	Average Annual Earnings
Atlanta, GA	$107,510
Chicago, IL	$121,370
Dallas-Fort Worth, TX	$112,420
Denver, CO	$95,670
Los Angeles, CA	$128,340
Minneapolis-St. Paul, MN	$107,170
New York, NY	$114,690
Phoenix, AZ	$91,580
San Francisco, CA	$122,870
Seattle, WA	$89,890

Average Earnings in Most Important Industries

Industry	Average Annual Earnings
Management of Companies and Enterprises	$124,760
Professional, Scientific, and Technical Services	$105,130
Insurance Carriers and Related Activities	$96,320
Administrative and Support Services	$94,720
Federal, State, and Local Government	$83,650

LIBRARIANS

- Average Earnings: $47,400
- Beginning Earnings: $29,740
- 25th Percentile: $38,000
- 75th Percentile: $58,520

Average Earnings in Major Metropolitan Areas

Metropolitan Area	Average Annual Earnings
Atlanta, GA	$56,090
Chicago, IL	$53,430
Dallas-Fort Worth, TX	$47,130
Denver, CO	$56,530
Los Angeles, CA	$56,530
Minneapolis-St. Paul, MN	$48,080
New York, NY	$53,090
Phoenix, AZ	$42,500
San Francisco, CA	$61,000
Seattle, WA	$55,820

Average Earnings in Most Important Industries

Industry	Average Annual Earnings
Professional, Scientific, and Technical Services	$54,080
Educational Services	$49,250
Federal, State, and Local Government	$44,330
Hospitals	$44,020
Other Information Services	$41,040

LIBRARY ASSISTANTS, CLERICAL

- Average Earnings: $21,140
- Beginning Earnings: $13,570
- 25th Percentile: $16,360
- 75th Percentile: $27,190

Average Earnings in Major Metropolitan Areas

Metropolitan Area	Average Annual Earnings
Atlanta, GA	$19,520
Chicago, IL	$23,670
Dallas-Fort Worth, TX	$21,970
Denver, CO	$21,650
Los Angeles, CA	$23,830
Minneapolis-St. Paul, MN	$24,720
New York, NY	$25,350
Phoenix, AZ	$26,730
San Francisco, CA	$32,470
Seattle, WA	$23,100

Average Earnings in Most Important Industries

Industry	Average Annual Earnings
Professional, Scientific, and Technical Services	$28,630
Hospitals	$24,650
Educational Services	$22,730
Other Information Services	$20,010
Federal, State, and Local Government	$19,970

LIBRARY TECHNICIANS

- Average Earnings: $25,650
- Beginning Earnings: $15,150
- 25th Percentile: $19,330
- 75th Percentile: $33,280

Average Earnings in Major Metropolitan Areas

Metropolitan Area	Average Annual Earnings
Atlanta, GA	$24,790
Chicago, IL	$24,020
Dallas-Fort Worth, TX	$26,100
Denver, CO	$29,130
Los Angeles, CA	$33,400
Minneapolis-St. Paul, MN	$35,260
New York, NY	$27,950
Phoenix, AZ	$25,950
San Francisco, CA	$39,250
Seattle, WA	$33,880

Average Earnings in Most Important Industries

Industry	Average Annual Earnings
Professional, Scientific, and Technical Services	$34,250
Museums, Historical Sites, and Similar Institutions	$29,030
Educational Services	$26,280
Federal, State, and Local Government	$24,890
Other Information Services	$23,660

LICENSED PRACTICAL AND LICENSED VOCATIONAL NURSES

- Average Earnings: $35,230
- Beginning Earnings: $25,340
- 25th Percentile: $29,970
- 75th Percentile: $42,180

Average Earnings in Major Metropolitan Areas

Metropolitan Area	Average Annual Earnings
Atlanta, GA	$33,550
Chicago, IL	$38,140
Dallas-Fort Worth, TX	$38,950
Denver, CO	$40,090
Los Angeles, CA	$41,650
Minneapolis-St. Paul, MN	$38,230
New York, NY	$43,220
Phoenix, AZ	$40,090
San Francisco, CA	$51,350
Seattle, WA	$41,580

Average Earnings in Most Important Industries

Industry	Average Annual Earnings
Administrative and Support Services	$41,270
Nursing and Residential Care Facilities	$36,850
Federal, State, and Local Government	$35,550
Hospitals	$33,820
Ambulatory Health Care Services	$33,540

LINE INSTALLERS AND REPAIRERS

- Average Earnings: $45,712
- Beginning Earnings: $25,965
- 25th Percentile: $34,253
- 75th Percentile: $56,760

Average Earnings in Major Metropolitan Areas

Metropolitan Area	Average Annual Earnings
Atlanta, GA	$38,454
Chicago, IL	$55,670
Dallas-Fort Worth, TX	$41,846
Denver, CO	$40,003
Los Angeles, CA	$43,480
Minneapolis-St. Paul, MN	$45,886
New York, NY	$62,360
Phoenix, AZ	$38,240
San Francisco, CA	$41,790
Seattle, WA	$50,162

Average Earnings in Most Important Industries

Industry	Average Annual Earnings
Utilities	$53,069
Telecommunications	$49,690
Specialty Trade Contractors	$36,884
Broadcasting (Except Internet)	$36,589
Heavy and Civil Engineering Construction	$35,502

LOAN OFFICERS

- Average Earnings: $49,440
- Beginning Earnings: $28,580
- 25th Percentile: $36,240
- 75th Percentile: $70,270

Average Earnings in Major Metropolitan Areas

Metropolitan Area	Average Annual Earnings
Atlanta, GA	$53,380
Chicago, IL	$52,310
Dallas-Fort Worth, TX	$58,770
Denver, CO	$48,970
Los Angeles, CA	$56,260
Minneapolis-St. Paul, MN	$54,890
New York, NY	$55,920
Phoenix, AZ	$52,990
San Francisco, CA	$64,260
Seattle, WA	$52,310

Average Earnings in Most Important Industries

Industry	Average Annual Earnings
Credit Intermediation and Related Activities	$49,120

LODGING MANAGERS

- Average Earnings: $40,610
- Beginning Earnings: $23,580
- 25th Percentile: $30,280
- 75th Percentile: $55,790

Average Earnings in Major Metropolitan Areas

Metropolitan Area	Average Annual Earnings
Atlanta, GA	$62,560
Chicago, IL	$53,060
Dallas-Fort Worth, TX	$43,080
Denver, CO	$59,890
Los Angeles, CA	$43,650
Minneapolis-St. Paul, MN	$43,600
New York, NY	$66,270
Phoenix, AZ	$40,900
San Francisco, CA	$44,540
Seattle, WA	$77,400

Average Earnings in Most Important Industries

Industry	Average Annual Earnings
Accommodation	$40,190

MACHINE SETTERS, OPERATORS, AND TENDERS—METAL AND PLASTIC

- Average Earnings: $28,425
- Beginning Earnings: $18,297
- 25th Percentile: $22,379
- 75th Percentile: $35,946

Average Earnings in Major Metropolitan Areas

Metropolitan Area	Average Annual Earnings
Atlanta, GA	$27,412
Chicago, IL	$26,906
Dallas-Fort Worth, TX	$24,116
Denver, CO	$28,395
Los Angeles, CA	$23,751
Minneapolis-St. Paul, MN	$32,012
New York, NY	$24,805
Phoenix, AZ	$26,016
San Francisco, CA	$29,539
Seattle, WA	$31,829

Average Earnings in Most Important Industries

Industry	Average Annual Earnings
Transportation Equipment Manufacturing	$31,513
Primary Metal Manufacturing	$30,476
Machinery Manufacturing	$30,323
Fabricated Metal Product Manufacturing	$27,788
Plastics and Rubber Products Manufacturing	$24,719

MACHINISTS

- Average Earnings: $34,350
- Beginning Earnings: $21,340
- 25th Percentile: $27,220
- 75th Percentile: $42,690

Average Earnings in Major Metropolitan Areas

Metropolitan Area	Average Annual Earnings
Atlanta, GA	$34,090
Chicago, IL	$32,520
Dallas-Fort Worth, TX	$31,500
Denver, CO	$40,050
Los Angeles, CA	$35,920
Minneapolis-St. Paul, MN	$40,710
New York, NY	$36,770
Phoenix, AZ	$34,240
San Francisco, CA	$43,330
Seattle, WA	$41,640

Average Earnings in Most Important Industries

Industry	Average Annual Earnings
Transportation Equipment Manufacturing	$36,430
Machinery Manufacturing	$35,320
Fabricated Metal Product Manufacturing	$33,310
Merchant Wholesalers, Durable Goods	$31,950
Administrative and Support Services	$26,210

MAINTENANCE AND REPAIR WORKERS, GENERAL

- Average Earnings: $31,210
- Beginning Earnings: $18,560
- 25th Percentile: $23,560
- 75th Percentile: $40,520

Average Earnings in Major Metropolitan Areas

Metropolitan Area	Average Annual Earnings
Atlanta, GA	$32,660
Chicago, IL	$37,330
Dallas-Fort Worth, TX	$29,030
Denver, CO	$32,250
Los Angeles, CA	$31,790
Minneapolis-St. Paul, MN	$37,570
New York, NY	$35,710
Phoenix, AZ	$29,240
San Francisco, CA	$41,010
Seattle, WA	$37,890

Average Earnings in Most Important Industries

Industry	Average Annual Earnings
Federal, State, and Local Government	$32,600
Educational Services	$31,630
Administrative and Support Services	$30,170
Real Estate	$26,600
Accommodation	$23,800

MANAGEMENT ANALYSTS

- Average Earnings: $66,380
- Beginning Earnings: $38,650
- 25th Percentile: $49,600
- 75th Percentile: $90,080

Average Earnings in Major Metropolitan Areas

Metropolitan Area	Average Annual Earnings
Atlanta, GA	$70,420
Chicago, IL	$68,190
Dallas-Fort Worth, TX	$65,890
Denver, CO	$73,060
Los Angeles, CA	$67,850
Minneapolis-St. Paul, MN	$66,620
New York, NY	$73,610
Phoenix, AZ	$56,790
San Francisco, CA	$75,800
Seattle, WA	$69,860

Average Earnings in Most Important Industries

Industry	Average Annual Earnings
Professional, Scientific, and Technical Services	$73,990
Management of Companies and Enterprises	$66,490
Administrative and Support Services	$65,460
Federal, State, and Local Government	$62,250
Insurance Carriers and Related Activities	$57,720

MARKET AND SURVEY RESEARCHERS

- Average Earnings: $54,694
- Beginning Earnings: $29,991
- 25th Percentile: $39,361
- 75th Percentile: $78,618

Average Earnings in Major Metropolitan Areas

Metropolitan Area	Average Annual Earnings
Atlanta, GA	$53,950
Chicago, IL	$51,779
Dallas-Fort Worth, TX	$57,081
Denver, CO	$68,018
Los Angeles, CA	$56,460
Minneapolis-St. Paul, MN	$59,663
New York, NY	$60,680
Phoenix, AZ	$45,976
San Francisco, CA	$67,861
Seattle, WA	$77,700

Average Earnings in Most Important Industries

Industry	Average Annual Earnings
Publishing Industries (Except Internet)	$67,044
Management of Companies and Enterprises	$59,203
Credit Intermediation and Related Activities	$55,210
Insurance Carriers and Related Activities	$54,360
Professional, Scientific, and Technical Services	$48,693

MASSAGE THERAPISTS

- Average Earnings: $32,890
- Beginning Earnings: $15,000
- 25th Percentile: $21,370
- 75th Percentile: $51,840

Average Earnings in Major Metropolitan Areas

Metropolitan Area	Average Annual Earnings
Atlanta, GA	$34,230
Chicago, IL	$41,760
Dallas-Fort Worth, TX	$27,330
Denver, CO	$30,530
Los Angeles, CA	$25,430
Minneapolis-St. Paul, MN	$34,220
New York, NY	$48,170
Phoenix, AZ	$30,730
San Francisco, CA	$32,250
Seattle, WA	$60,660

Average Earnings in Most Important Industries

Industry	Average Annual Earnings
Hospitals	$39,140
Ambulatory Health Care Services	$38,950
Personal and Laundry Services	$29,730
Amusement, Gambling, and Recreation Industries	$38,400
Accommodation	$22,770

MATERIAL MOVING OCCUPATIONS

- Average Earnings: $22,251
- Beginning Earnings: $15,286
- 25th Percentile: $18,001
- 75th Percentile: $28,356

Average Earnings in Major Metropolitan Areas

Metropolitan Area	Average Annual Earnings
Atlanta, GA	$22,017
Chicago, IL	$22,055
Dallas-Fort Worth, TX	$21,021
Denver, CO	$23,403
Los Angeles, CA	$20,764
Minneapolis-St. Paul, MN	$27,716
New York, NY	$22,846
Phoenix, AZ	$20,407
San Francisco, CA	$25,994
Seattle, WA	$24,706

Average Earnings in Most Important Industries

Industry	Average Annual Earnings
Warehousing and Storage	$25,506
Merchant Wholesalers, Durable Goods	$23,654
Merchant Wholesalers, Nondurable Goods	$23,187
Administrative and Support Services	$18,107
Food and Beverage Stores	$16,206

MATHEMATICIANS

- Average Earnings: $80,920
- Beginning Earnings: $41,750
- 25th Percentile: $57,530
- 75th Percentile: $102,200

Average Earnings in Major Metropolitan Areas

Metropolitan Area	Average Annual Earnings
Chicago, IL	$75,380

Average Earnings in Most Important Industries

Industry	Average Annual Earnings
Professional, Scientific, and Technical Services	$87,460
Federal, State, and Local Government	$84,720

MEDICAL AND HEALTH SERVICES MANAGERS

- Average Earnings: $69,700
- Beginning Earnings: $43,640
- 25th Percentile: $54,620
- 75th Percentile: $90,050

Average Earnings in Major Metropolitan Areas

Metropolitan Area	Average Annual Earnings
Atlanta, GA	$63,880
Chicago, IL	$67,230
Dallas-Fort Worth, TX	$61,120
Denver, CO	$78,600
Los Angeles, CA	$84,770
Minneapolis-St. Paul, MN	$78,610
New York, NY	$86,710
Phoenix, AZ	$59,510
San Francisco, CA	$95,030
Seattle, WA	$94,510

Average Earnings in Most Important Industries

Industry	Average Annual Earnings
Educational Services	$76,050
Hospitals	$73,600
Federal, State, and Local Government	$73,320
Ambulatory Health Care Services	$65,520
Nursing and Residential Care Facilities	$59,780

MEDICAL ASSISTANTS

- Average Earnings: $25,350
- Beginning Earnings: $18,330
- 25th Percentile: $21,150
- 75th Percentile: $30,130

Average Earnings in Major Metropolitan Areas

Metropolitan Area	Average Annual Earnings
Atlanta, GA	$26,680
Chicago, IL	$26,970
Dallas-Fort Worth, TX	$25,890
Denver, CO	$30,980
Los Angeles, CA	$27,730
Minneapolis-St. Paul, MN	$29,200
New York, NY	$28,580
Phoenix, AZ	$26,640
San Francisco, CA	$32,520
Seattle, WA	$32,370

Average Earnings in Most Important Industries

Industry	Average Annual Earnings
Educational Services	$26,700
Administrative and Support Services	$26,530
Hospitals	$25,750
Ambulatory Health Care Services	$25,240
Nursing and Residential Care Facilities	$23,620

MEDICAL RECORDS AND HEALTH INFORMATION TECHNICIANS

- Average Earnings: $26,690
- Beginning Earnings: $18,410
- 25th Percentile: $21,480
- 75th Percentile: $34,210

Average Earnings in Major Metropolitan Areas

Metropolitan Area	Average Annual Earnings
Atlanta, GA	$27,610
Chicago, IL	$26,200
Dallas-Fort Worth, TX	$26,070
Denver, CO	$31,370
Los Angeles, CA	$27,660
Minneapolis-St. Paul, MN	$31,050
New York, NY	$36,380
Phoenix, AZ	$26,170
San Francisco, CA	$37,770
Seattle, WA	$30,550

Average Earnings in Most Important Industries

Industry	Average Annual Earnings
Professional, Scientific, and Technical Services	$33,750
Federal, State, and Local Government	$33,710
Hospitals	$27,870
Nursing and Residential Care Facilities	$26,930
Ambulatory Health Care Services	$23,850

MEDICAL SCIENTISTS

- Average Earnings: $61,281
- Beginning Earnings: $35,326
- 25th Percentile: $44,723
- 75th Percentile: $85,361

Average Earnings in Major Metropolitan Areas

Metropolitan Area	Average Annual Earnings
Atlanta, GA	$79,977
Chicago, IL	$55,430
Dallas-Fort Worth, TX	$56,930
Denver, CO	$89,190
Los Angeles, CA	$66,070
Minneapolis-St. Paul, MN	$50,910
New York, NY	$70,232
Phoenix, AZ	$51,530
San Francisco, CA	$77,558
Seattle, WA	$61,090

Average Earnings in Most Important Industries

Industry	Average Annual Earnings
Chemical Manufacturing	$76,050
Federal, State, and Local Government	$70,700
Professional, Scientific, and Technical Services	$68,499
Hospitals	$57,637
Educational Services	$45,217

MEDICAL TRANSCRIPTIONISTS

- Average Earnings: $29,080
- Beginning Earnings: $20,710
- 25th Percentile: $24,580
- 75th Percentile: $34,640

Average Earnings in Major Metropolitan Areas

Metropolitan Area	Average Annual Earnings
Atlanta, GA	$31,720
Chicago, IL	$31,560
Dallas-Fort Worth, TX	$31,250
Denver, CO	$35,190
Los Angeles, CA	$40,150
Minneapolis-St. Paul, MN	$32,900
New York, NY	$35,460
Phoenix, AZ	$30,890
San Francisco, CA	$40,840
Seattle, WA	$35,850

Average Earnings in Most Important Industries

Industry	Average Annual Earnings
Hospitals	$29,530
Administrative and Support Services	$28,820
Ambulatory Health Care Services	$28,430

MEDICAL, DENTAL, AND OPHTHALMIC LABORATORY TECHNICIANS

- Average Earnings: $29,417
- Beginning Earnings: $17,991
- 25th Percentile: $22,423
- 75th Percentile: $38,348

Average Earnings in Major Metropolitan Areas

Metropolitan Area	Average Annual Earnings
Atlanta, GA	$33,404
Chicago, IL	$30,907
Dallas-Fort Worth, TX	$25,542
Los Angeles, CA	$29,729
Minneapolis-St. Paul, MN	$34,916
New York, NY	$34,745
Phoenix, AZ	$29,450
San Francisco, CA	$36,318
Seattle, WA	$39,658

Average Earnings in Most Important Industries

Industry	Average Annual Earnings
Hospitals	$32,351
Ambulatory Health Care Services	$32,242
Miscellaneous Manufacturing	$29,361
Merchant Wholesalers, Durable Goods	$26,581
Health and Personal Care Stores	$24,064

MEETING AND CONVENTION PLANNERS

- Average Earnings: $41,280
- Beginning Earnings: $25,200
- 25th Percentile: $32,050
- 75th Percentile: $53,820

Average Earnings in Major Metropolitan Areas

Metropolitan Area	Average Annual Earnings
Atlanta, GA	$41,650
Chicago, IL	$52,420
Dallas-Fort Worth, TX	$41,820
Denver, CO	$42,090
Los Angeles, CA	$43,010
Minneapolis-St. Paul, MN	$44,170
New York, NY	$48,790
Phoenix, AZ	$43,710
San Francisco, CA	$48,460
Seattle, WA	$43,150

Average Earnings in Most Important Industries

Industry	Average Annual Earnings
Professional, Scientific, and Technical Services	$44,510
Religious, Grantmaking, Civic, Professional, and Similar Organizations	$43,670
Federal, State, and Local Government	$41,390
Educational Services	$38,420
Accommodation	$37,780

METER READERS, UTILITIES

- Average Earnings: $29,310
- Beginning Earnings: $18,520
- 25th Percentile: $22,640
- 75th Percentile: $38,330

Average Earnings in Major Metropolitan Areas

Metropolitan Area	Average Annual Earnings
Atlanta, GA	$29,670
Chicago, IL	$40,660
Dallas-Fort Worth, TX	$26,430
Minneapolis-St. Paul, MN	$46,330
Phoenix, AZ	$47,120
Seattle, WA	$39,570

Average Earnings in Most Important Industries

Industry	Average Annual Earnings
Utilities	$33,520
Federal, State, and Local Government	$27,350
Administrative and Support Services	$24,890

MILLWRIGHTS

- Average Earnings: $44,780
- Beginning Earnings: $28,510
- 25th Percentile: $35,290
- 75th Percentile: $58,700

Average Earnings in Major Metropolitan Areas

Metropolitan Area	Average Annual Earnings
Atlanta, GA	$43,130
Chicago, IL	$57,990
Dallas-Fort Worth, TX	$38,380
Minneapolis-St. Paul, MN	$52,740
New York, NY	$58,110
Phoenix, AZ	$48,560
San Francisco, CA	$63,620
Seattle, WA	$45,370

Average Earnings in Most Important Industries

Industry	Average Annual Earnings
Transportation Equipment Manufacturing	$61,860
Primary Metal Manufacturing	$43,060
Specialty Trade Contractors	$40,510
Construction of Buildings	$39,810
Wood Product Manufacturing	$35,920

MUSICIANS, SINGERS, AND RELATED WORKERS

- Average Earnings: $34,810
- Beginning Earnings: $16,330
- 25th Percentile: $23,710
- 75th Percentile: $50,980

Average Earnings in Major Metropolitan Areas

Metropolitan Area	Average Annual Earnings
Chicago, IL	$38,720
New York, NY	$36,250
San Francisco, CA	$43,420
Seattle, WA	$61,800

Average Earnings in Most Important Industries

Industry	Average Annual Earnings
Motion Picture and Sound Recording Industries	$52,250
Broadcasting (Except Internet)	$42,560
Educational Services	$41,180
Religious, Grantmaking, Civic, Professional, and Similar Organizations	$34,500
Performing Arts, Spectator Sports, and Related Industries	$32,700

Note: Figures apply only to Music Directors and Composers.

NEWS ANALYSTS, REPORTERS, AND CORRESPONDENTS

- Average Earnings: $33,451
- Beginning Earnings: $18,559
- 25th Percentile: $23,834
- 75th Percentile: $53,872

Average Earnings in Major Metropolitan Areas

Metropolitan Area	Average Annual Earnings
Atlanta, GA	$44,730
Dallas-Fort Worth, TX	$40,130
Denver, CO	$42,570
Los Angeles, CA	$58,517
Minneapolis-St. Paul, MN	$54,644
New York, NY	$46,705
San Francisco, CA	$52,360

Average Earnings in Most Important Industries

Industry	Average Annual Earnings
Other Information Services	$57,050
Professional, Scientific, and Technical Services	$47,923
Broadcasting (Except Internet)	$40,901
Federal, State, and Local Government	$33,410
Publishing Industries (Except Internet)	$30,161

NUCLEAR MEDICINE TECHNOLOGISTS

- Average Earnings: $59,670
- Beginning Earnings: $44,650
- 25th Percentile: $50,980
- 75th Percentile: $69,760

Average Earnings in Major Metropolitan Areas

Metropolitan Area	Average Annual Earnings
Atlanta, GA	$57,340
Chicago, IL	$66,630
Dallas-Fort Worth, TX	$61,190
Denver, CO	$61,450
Los Angeles, CA	$64,440
Minneapolis-St. Paul, MN	$63,880
New York, NY	$66,790
Phoenix, AZ	$58,050
San Francisco, CA	$75,440
Seattle, WA	$69,660

Average Earnings in Most Important Industries

Industry	Average Annual Earnings
Management of Companies and Enterprises	$77,050
Administrative and Support Services	$74,640
Ambulatory Health Care Services	$62,020
Hospitals	$58,110
Federal, State, and Local Government	$57,280

NURSING, PSYCHIATRIC, AND HOME HEALTH AIDES

- Average Earnings: $20,650
- Beginning Earnings: $15,129
- 25th Percentile: $17,615
- 75th Percentile: $24,640

Average Earnings in Major Metropolitan Areas

Metropolitan Area	Average Annual Earnings
Atlanta, GA	$20,692
Chicago, IL	$20,669
Dallas-Fort Worth, TX	$19,663
Denver, CO	$24,975
Los Angeles, CA	$20,666
Minneapolis-St. Paul, MN	$25,130
New York, NY	$24,150
Phoenix, AZ	$21,306
San Francisco, CA	$25,219
Seattle, WA	$24,302

Average Earnings in Most Important Industries

Industry	Average Annual Earnings
Federal, State, and Local Government	$25,130
Hospitals	$22,169
Nursing and Residential Care Facilities	$20,227
Ambulatory Health Care Services	$19,038
Social Assistance	$18,865

OCCUPATIONAL HEALTH AND SAFETY SPECIALISTS AND TECHNICIANS

- Average Earnings: $51,477
- Beginning Earnings: $30,707
- 25th Percentile: $39,433
- 75th Percentile: $66,376

Average Earnings in Major Metropolitan Areas

Metropolitan Area	Average Annual Earnings
Atlanta, GA	$59,043
Chicago, IL	$57,271
Dallas-Fort Worth, TX	$47,510
Denver, CO	$66,649
Los Angeles, CA	$47,840
Minneapolis-St. Paul, MN	$60,069
New York, NY	$55,881
Phoenix, AZ	$59,713
San Francisco, CA	$70,684
Seattle, WA	$58,460

Average Earnings in Most Important Industries

Industry	Average Annual Earnings
Transportation Equipment Manufacturing	$57,241
Professional, Scientific, and Technical Services	$55,390
Federal, State, and Local Government	$50,112
Hospitals	$48,143
Educational Services	$46,008

OCCUPATIONAL THERAPIST ASSISTANTS AND AIDES

- Average Earnings: $36,366
- Beginning Earnings: $22,871
- 25th Percentile: $29,570
- 75th Percentile: $43,582

Average Earnings in Major Metropolitan Areas

Metropolitan Area	Average Annual Earnings
Atlanta, GA	$29,253
Chicago, IL	$33,210
Dallas-Fort Worth, TX	$45,560
Denver, CO	$35,920
Los Angeles, CA	$41,460
Minneapolis-St. Paul, MN	$34,720
New York, NY	$39,832
Phoenix, AZ	$31,082
San Francisco, CA	$50,370
Seattle, WA	$34,047

Average Earnings in Most Important Industries

Industry	Average Annual Earnings
Ambulatory Health Care Services	$39,024
Nursing and Residential Care Facilities	$37,239
Hospitals	$34,464
Educational Services	$33,124
Social Assistance	$26,698

OCCUPATIONAL THERAPISTS

- Average Earnings: $56,860
- Beginning Earnings: $38,840
- 25th Percentile: $47,590
- 75th Percentile: $69,740

Average Earnings in Major Metropolitan Areas

Metropolitan Area	Average Annual Earnings
Atlanta, GA	$53,820
Chicago, IL	$59,050
Dallas-Fort Worth, TX	$60,250
Denver, CO	$50,420
Los Angeles, CA	$68,680
Minneapolis-St. Paul, MN	$51,510
New York, NY	$59,290
Phoenix, AZ	$44,080
San Francisco, CA	$76,940
Seattle, WA	$56,760

Average Earnings in Most Important Industries

Industry	Average Annual Earnings
Ambulatory Health Care Services	$59,440
Nursing and Residential Care Facilities	$58,380
Hospitals	$57,630
Educational Services	$51,250
Social Assistance	$49,930

OFFICE AND ADMINISTRATIVE SUPPORT WORKER SUPERVISORS AND MANAGERS

- Average Earnings: $42,400
- Beginning Earnings: $25,950
- 25th Percentile: $32,910
- 75th Percentile: $54,630

Average Earnings in Major Metropolitan Areas

Metropolitan Area	Average Annual Earnings
Atlanta, GA	$41,960
Chicago, IL	$44,880
Dallas-Fort Worth, TX	$44,190
Denver, CO	$48,430
Los Angeles, CA	$46,730
Minneapolis-St. Paul, MN	$45,280
New York, NY	$50,170
Phoenix, AZ	$42,590
San Francisco, CA	$50,510
Seattle, WA	$50,380

Average Earnings in Most Important Industries

Industry	Average Annual Earnings
Federal, State, and Local Government	$46,240
Professional, Scientific, and Technical Services	$46,240
Credit Intermediation and Related Activities	$40,430
Ambulatory Health Care Services	$40,680
Administrative and Support Services	$38,810

OFFICE CLERKS, GENERAL

- Average Earnings: $23,070
- Beginning Earnings: $14,530
- 25th Percentile: $18,270
- 75th Percentile: $29,420

Average Earnings in Major Metropolitan Areas

Metropolitan Area	Average Annual Earnings
Atlanta, GA	$23,450
Chicago, IL	$24,340
Dallas-Fort Worth, TX	$23,700
Denver, CO	$27,670
Los Angeles, CA	$24,070
Minneapolis-St. Paul, MN	$26,910
New York, NY	$26,050
San Francisco, CA	$28,340
Seattle, WA	$27,350

Average Earnings in Most Important Industries

Industry	Average Annual Earnings
Federal, State, and Local Government	$26,730
Educational Services	$23,100
Ambulatory Health Care Services	$23,020
Professional, Scientific, and Technical Services	$22,960
Administrative and Support Services	$21,340

OPERATIONS RESEARCH ANALYSTS

- Average Earnings: $62,180
- Beginning Earnings: $37,310
- 25th Percentile: $47,400
- 75th Percentile: $81,350

Average Earnings in Major Metropolitan Areas

Metropolitan Area	Average Annual Earnings
Atlanta, GA	$53,580
Chicago, IL	$63,580
Denver, CO	$60,450
Los Angeles, CA	$64,220
Minneapolis-St. Paul, MN	$49,550
New York, NY	$70,060
Phoenix, AZ	$53,760
San Francisco, CA	$69,920
Seattle, WA	$67,250

Average Earnings in Most Important Industries

Industry	Average Annual Earnings
Federal, State, and Local Government	$67,910
Professional, Scientific, and Technical Services	$65,990
Internet Service Providers, Web Search Portals, and Data Processing Service	$65,310
Insurance Carriers and Related Activities	$54,880
Credit Intermediation and Related Activities	$51,490

OPTICIANS, DISPENSING

- Average Earnings: $29,000
- Beginning Earnings: $18,490
- 25th Percentile: $22,470
- 75th Percentile: $36,920

Average Earnings in Major Metropolitan Areas

Metropolitan Area	Average Annual Earnings
Atlanta, GA	$32,300
Chicago, IL	$27,440
Dallas-Fort Worth, TX	$26,030
Denver, CO	$34,440
Los Angeles, CA	$33,310
Minneapolis-St. Paul, MN	$32,110
New York, NY	$44,890
Phoenix, AZ	$29,490
San Francisco, CA	$33,660
Seattle, WA	$37,690

Average Earnings in Most Important Industries

Industry	Average Annual Earnings
Health and Personal Care Stores	$30,830
Ambulatory Health Care Services	$29,080

OPTOMETRISTS

- Average Earnings: $88,040
- Beginning Earnings: $42,860
- 25th Percentile: $64,400
- 75th Percentile: $114,600

Average Earnings in Major Metropolitan Areas

Metropolitan Area	Average Annual Earnings
Chicago, IL	$87,260
Dallas-Fort Worth, TX	$87,240
Los Angeles, CA	$65,810
Minneapolis-St. Paul, MN	$107,410
New York, NY	$100,810
Phoenix, AZ	$93,320
San Francisco, CA	$102,110
Seattle, WA	$99,780

Average Earnings in Most Important Industries

Industry	Average Annual Earnings
Health and Personal Care Stores	$93,940
Federal, State, and Local Government	$92,340
Ambulatory Health Care Services	$87,650
Hospitals	$68,510
Educational Services	$59,880

ORDER CLERKS

- Average Earnings: $25,570
- Beginning Earnings: $16,530
- 25th Percentile: $20,040
- 75th Percentile: $33,020

Average Earnings in Major Metropolitan Areas

Metropolitan Area	Average Annual Earnings
Atlanta, GA	$27,330
Chicago, IL	$26,380
Dallas-Fort Worth, TX	$25,920
Denver, CO	$29,190
Los Angeles, CA	$26,450
Minneapolis-St. Paul, MN	$31,090
New York, NY	$30,480
Phoenix, AZ	$24,860
San Francisco, CA	$31,410
Seattle, WA	$32,070

Average Earnings in Most Important Industries

Industry	Average Annual Earnings
Telecommunications	$41,950
Merchant Wholesalers, Durable Goods	$27,910
Wholesale Electronic Markets and Agents and Brokers	$26,750
Merchant Wholesalers, Nondurable Goods	$25,920
Nonstore Retailers	$21,490

PAINTERS AND PAPERHANGERS

- Average Earnings: $30,879
- Beginning Earnings: $19,949
- 25th Percentile: $24,547
- 75th Percentile: $40,499

Average Earnings in Major Metropolitan Areas

Metropolitan Area	Average Annual Earnings
Atlanta, GA	$28,560
Chicago, IL	$44,820
Dallas-Fort Worth, TX	$27,070
Denver, CO	$32,500
Los Angeles, CA	$31,460
Minneapolis-St. Paul, MN	$34,590
New York, NY	$40,696
Phoenix, AZ	$28,438
San Francisco, CA	$41,820
Seattle, WA	$38,270

Average Earnings in Most Important Industries

Industry	Average Annual Earnings
Federal, State, and Local Government	$40,890
Construction of Buildings	$31,570
Specialty Trade Contractors	$30,191
Administrative and Support Services	$27,490
Real Estate	$27,040

PAINTING AND COATING WORKERS, EXCEPT CONSTRUCTION AND MAINTENANCE

- Average Earnings: $28,424
- Beginning Earnings: $18,563
- 25th Percentile: $22,428
- 75th Percentile: $36,715

Average Earnings in Major Metropolitan Areas

Metropolitan Area	Average Annual Earnings
Atlanta, GA	$34,053
Chicago, IL	$31,066
Dallas-Fort Worth, TX	$27,453
Denver, CO	$35,151
Los Angeles, CA	$26,421
Minneapolis-St. Paul, MN	$35,836
New York, NY	$29,379
Phoenix, AZ	$26,235
San Francisco, CA	$36,814
Seattle, WA	$41,952

Average Earnings in Most Important Industries

Industry	Average Annual Earnings
Repair and Maintenance	$34,424
Transportation Equipment Manufacturing	$33,385
Machinery Manufacturing	$28,088
Fabricated Metal Product Manufacturing	$25,657
Furniture and Related Product Manufacturing	$23,693

PARALEGALS AND LEGAL ASSISTANTS

- Average Earnings: $41,817
- Beginning Earnings: $26,952
- 25th Percentile: $33,309
- 75th Percentile: $52,871

Average Earnings in Major Metropolitan Areas

Metropolitan Area	Average Annual Earnings
Atlanta, GA	$44,974
Chicago, IL	$42,806
Dallas-Fort Worth, TX	$41,385
Denver, CO	$43,282
Los Angeles, CA	$49,871
Minneapolis-St. Paul, MN	$46,444
New York, NY	$47,180
Phoenix, AZ	$44,660
San Francisco, CA	$51,790
Seattle, WA	$47,002

Average Earnings in Most Important Industries

Industry	Average Annual Earnings
Federal, State, and Local Government	$43,995
Professional, Scientific, and Technical Services	$40,088

PAYROLL AND TIMEKEEPING CLERKS

- Average Earnings: $31,360
- Beginning Earnings: $20,190
- 25th Percentile: $25,110
- 75th Percentile: $38,190

Average Earnings in Major Metropolitan Areas

Metropolitan Area	Average Annual Earnings
Atlanta, GA	$32,620
Chicago, IL	$33,080
Dallas-Fort Worth, TX	$30,480
Denver, CO	$36,370
Los Angeles, CA	$35,130
Minneapolis-St. Paul, MN	$35,940
New York, NY	$36,990
Phoenix, AZ	$30,550
San Francisco, CA	$42,410
Seattle, WA	$38,450

Average Earnings in Most Important Industries

Industry	Average Annual Earnings
Federal, State, and Local Government	$34,040
Educational Services	$33,030
Professional, Scientific, and Technical Services	$32,990
Specialty Trade Contractors	$30,670
Administrative and Support Services	$29,430

PERSONAL AND HOME CARE AIDES

- Average Earnings: $17,340
- Beginning Earnings: $12,480
- 25th Percentile: $14,490
- 75th Percentile: $20,650

Average Earnings in Major Metropolitan Areas

Metropolitan Area	Average Annual Earnings
Atlanta, GA	$20,120
Chicago, IL	$16,750
Dallas-Fort Worth, TX	$13,560
Denver, CO	$18,540
Los Angeles, CA	$18,600
Minneapolis-St. Paul, MN	$21,110
New York, NY	$19,900
Phoenix, AZ	$19,670
San Francisco, CA	$21,820

Average Earnings in Most Important Industries

Industry	Average Annual Earnings
Administrative and Support Services	$19,980
Federal, State, and Local Government	$19,860
Nursing and Residential Care Facilities	$19,020
Social Assistance	$18,280
Ambulatory Health Care Services	$14,970

PEST CONTROL WORKERS

- Average Earnings: $27,170
- Beginning Earnings: $17,590
- 25th Percentile: $21,730
- 75th Percentile: $34,380

Average Earnings in Major Metropolitan Areas

Metropolitan Area	Average Annual Earnings
Atlanta, GA	$27,470
Chicago, IL	$33,020
Dallas-Fort Worth, TX	$34,810
Denver, CO	$29,590
Los Angeles, CA	$27,800
Minneapolis-St. Paul, MN	$37,100
New York, NY	$30,130
Phoenix, AZ	$24,260
San Francisco, CA	$31,470

Average Earnings in Most Important Industries

Industry	Average Annual Earnings
Administrative and Support Services	$27,110

PHARMACISTS

- Average Earnings: $89,820
- Beginning Earnings: $64,350
- 25th Percentile: $78,620
- 75th Percentile: $103,300

Average Earnings in Major Metropolitan Areas

Metropolitan Area	Average Annual Earnings
Atlanta, GA	$90,570
Chicago, IL	$87,550
Dallas-Fort Worth, TX	$98,450
Denver, CO	$92,420
Los Angeles, CA	$101,000
Minneapolis-St. Paul, MN	$96,510
New York, NY	$88,430
Phoenix, AZ	$92,050
San Francisco, CA	$107,210
Seattle, WA	$87,110

Average Earnings in Most Important Industries

Industry	Average Annual Earnings
General Merchandise Stores	$92,790
Health and Personal Care Stores	$90,880
Food and Beverage Stores	$90,820
Hospitals	$88,120
Federal, State, and Local Government	$85,150

PHARMACY AIDES

- Average Earnings: $18,900
- Beginning Earnings: $13,850
- 25th Percentile: $15,770
- 75th Percentile: $23,340

Average Earnings in Major Metropolitan Areas

Metropolitan Area	Average Annual Earnings
Atlanta, GA	$17,600
Dallas-Fort Worth, TX	$19,810
Denver, CO	$26,540
Los Angeles, CA	$20,710
Minneapolis-St. Paul, MN	$19,930
New York, NY	$20,710
Phoenix, AZ	$23,600
San Francisco, CA	$26,810
Seattle, WA	$23,230

Average Earnings in Most Important Industries

Industry	Average Annual Earnings
Ambulatory Health Care Services	$24,210
Hospitals	$23,220
Merchant Wholesalers, Nondurable Goods	$21,000
Food and Beverage Stores	$20,500
Health and Personal Care Stores	$17,760

PHARMACY TECHNICIANS

- Average Earnings: $24,390
- Beginning Earnings: $17,100
- 25th Percentile: $20,080
- 75th Percentile: $29,650

Average Earnings in Major Metropolitan Areas

Metropolitan Area	Average Annual Earnings
Atlanta, GA	$23,040
Chicago, IL	$23,940
Dallas-Fort Worth, TX	$27,000
Denver, CO	$29,000
Los Angeles, CA	$31,700
Minneapolis-St. Paul, MN	$27,940
New York, NY	$26,220
Phoenix, AZ	$26,160
San Francisco, CA	$35,930
Seattle, WA	$32,960

Average Earnings in Most Important Industries

Industry	Average Annual Earnings
Ambulatory Health Care Services	$28,830
Hospitals	$27,590
Food and Beverage Stores	$25,210
General Merchandise Stores	$22,940
Health and Personal Care Stores	$22,730

PHOTOGRAPHERS

- Average Earnings: $26,100
- Beginning Earnings: $15,240
- 25th Percentile: $18,420
- 75th Percentile: $37,370

Average Earnings in Major Metropolitan Areas

Metropolitan Area	Average Annual Earnings
Atlanta, GA	$23,140
Chicago, IL	$27,480
Dallas-Fort Worth, TX	$18,890
Denver, CO	$40,790
Los Angeles, CA	$31,240
Minneapolis-St. Paul, MN	$41,200
New York, NY	$32,730
Phoenix, AZ	$30,200
San Francisco, CA	$45,910
Seattle, WA	$42,970

Average Earnings in Most Important Industries

Industry	Average Annual Earnings
Educational Services	$37,030
Publishing Industries (Except Internet)	$33,360
Broadcasting (Except Internet)	$32,300
Personal and Laundry Services	$24,080
Professional, Scientific, and Technical Services	$22,780

PHOTOGRAPHIC PROCESS WORKERS AND PROCESSING MACHINE OPERATORS

- Average Earnings: $20,145
- Beginning Earnings: $14,660
- 25th Percentile: $16,537
- 75th Percentile: $25,745

Average Earnings in Major Metropolitan Areas

Metropolitan Area	Average Annual Earnings
Atlanta, GA	$22,095
Chicago, IL	$22,884
Dallas-Fort Worth, TX	$22,810
Denver, CO	$20,948
Los Angeles, CA	$21,997
Minneapolis-St. Paul, MN	$23,997
New York, NY	$24,630
Phoenix, AZ	$21,520
San Francisco, CA	$25,573
Seattle, WA	$21,128

Average Earnings in Most Important Industries

Industry	Average Annual Earnings
Printing and Related Support Activities	$27,491
Professional, Scientific, and Technical Services	$22,514
Personal and Laundry Services	$21,911
Electronics and Appliance Stores	$19,590
Health and Personal Care Stores	$16,796

PHYSICAL THERAPIST ASSISTANTS AND AIDES

- Average Earnings: $31,996
- Beginning Earnings: $21,447
- 25th Percentile: $26,456
- 75th Percentile: $37,657

Average Earnings in Major Metropolitan Areas

Metropolitan Area	Average Annual Earnings
Atlanta, GA	$36,004
Chicago, IL	$32,024
Dallas-Fort Worth, TX	$33,073
Denver, CO	$29,779
Los Angeles, CA	$36,822
Minneapolis-St. Paul, MN	$32,739
New York, NY	$31,840
Phoenix, AZ	$26,136
San Francisco, CA	$39,754
Seattle, WA	$33,820

Average Earnings in Most Important Industries

Industry	Average Annual Earnings
Administrative and Support Services	$40,294
Federal, State, and Local Government	$36,251
Nursing and Residential Care Facilities	$34,381
Hospitals	$32,444
Ambulatory Health Care Services	$30,724

PHYSICAL THERAPISTS

- Average Earnings: $63,080
- Beginning Earnings: $44,750
- 25th Percentile: $52,270
- 75th Percentile: $74,530

Average Earnings in Major Metropolitan Areas

Metropolitan Area	Average Annual Earnings
Atlanta, GA	$64,010
Chicago, IL	$62,990
Dallas-Fort Worth, TX	$70,020
Denver, CO	$56,650
Los Angeles, CA	$68,060
Minneapolis-St. Paul, MN	$57,340
New York, NY	$68,660
Phoenix, AZ	$60,810
San Francisco, CA	$77,120
Seattle, WA	$61,430

Average Earnings in Most Important Industries

Industry	Average Annual Earnings
Administrative and Support Services	$66,510
Nursing and Residential Care Facilities	$64,520
Ambulatory Health Care Services	$63,770
Hospitals	$62,660
Educational Services	$56,320

PHYSICIAN ASSISTANTS

- Average Earnings: $72,030
- Beginning Earnings: $38,370
- 25th Percentile: $59,260
- 75th Percentile: $86,530

Average Earnings in Major Metropolitan Areas

Metropolitan Area	Average Annual Earnings
Atlanta, GA	$72,960
Chicago, IL	$40,640
Denver, CO	$69,940
Los Angeles, CA	$83,050
Minneapolis-St. Paul, MN	$76,300
New York, NY	$77,650
Phoenix, AZ	$72,390
San Francisco, CA	$83,950
Seattle, WA	$79,320

Average Earnings in Most Important Industries

Industry	Average Annual Earnings
Administrative and Support Services	$79,600
Federal, State, and Local Government	$73,910
Hospitals	$73,110
Ambulatory Health Care Services	$71,360
Educational Services	$68,980

PHYSICIANS AND SURGEONS

- Average Earnings: $91,658
- Beginning Earnings: $67,446
- 25th Percentile: $80,438
- 75th Percentile: $145,600

Average Earnings in Major Metropolitan Areas

Metropolitan Area	Average Annual Earnings
Atlanta, GA	$143,134
Chicago, IL	$133,244
Dallas-Fort Worth, TX	$145,600
Denver, CO	$145,600
Los Angeles, CA	$144,128
Minneapolis-St. Paul, MN	$143,804
New York, NY	$134,609
Phoenix, AZ	$139,575
San Francisco, CA	$135,997
Seattle, WA	$145,048

Average Earnings in Most Important Industries

Industry	Average Annual Earnings
Ambulatory Health Care Services	$145,229
Administrative and Support Services	$123,475
Federal, State, and Local Government	$119,700
Hospitals	$115,652
Educational Services	$55,766

PHYSICISTS AND ASTRONOMERS

- Average Earnings: $90,704
- Beginning Earnings: $49,121
- 25th Percentile: $67,061
- 75th Percentile: $113,462

Average Earnings in Major Metropolitan Areas

Metropolitan Area	Average Annual Earnings
Atlanta, GA	$92,340
Chicago, IL	$95,220
Dallas-Fort Worth, TX	$99,320
Los Angeles, CA	$105,040
Minneapolis-St. Paul, MN	$91,330
New York, NY	$94,200

Average Earnings in Most Important Industries

Industry	Average Annual Earnings
Hospitals	$111,840
Federal, State, and Local Government	$99,342
Computer and Electronic Product Manufacturing	$95,280
Professional, Scientific, and Technical Services	$91,650
Educational Services	$59,504

PIPELAYERS, PLUMBERS, PIPEFITTERS, AND STEAMFITTERS

- Average Earnings: $40,579
- Beginning Earnings: $24,092
- 25th Percentile: $30,791
- 75th Percentile: $53,938

Average Earnings in Major Metropolitan Areas

Metropolitan Area	Average Annual Earnings
Atlanta, GA	$34,650
Chicago, IL	$66,270
Dallas-Fort Worth, TX	$36,185
Denver, CO	$40,492
Los Angeles, CA	$42,160
Minneapolis-St. Paul, MN	$57,536
New York, NY	$61,160
Phoenix, AZ	$32,947
San Francisco, CA	$58,767
Seattle, WA	$53,837

Average Earnings in Most Important Industries

Industry	Average Annual Earnings
Transportation Equipment Manufacturing	$47,370
Specialty Trade Contractors	$41,534
Construction of Buildings	$40,761
Federal, State, and Local Government	$35,139
Heavy and Civil Engineering Construction	$33,053

PLASTERERS AND STUCCO MASONS

- Average Earnings: $33,440
- Beginning Earnings: $21,060
- 25th Percentile: $26,670
- 75th Percentile: $43,320

Average Earnings in Major Metropolitan Areas

Metropolitan Area	Average Annual Earnings
Chicago, IL	$53,620
Dallas-Fort Worth, TX	$33,700
Denver, CO	$30,540
Los Angeles, CA	$32,350
Minneapolis-St. Paul, MN	$61,730
New York, NY	$52,990
Phoenix, AZ	$26,760
San Francisco, CA	$55,300
Seattle, WA	$60,450

Average Earnings in Most Important Industries

Industry	Average Annual Earnings
Specialty Trade Contractors	$33,330

PODIATRISTS

- Average Earnings: $100,550
- Beginning Earnings: $43,990
- 25th Percentile: $67,010
- 75th Percentile: $145,600

Average Earnings in Major Metropolitan Areas

Metropolitan Area	Average Annual Earnings
Atlanta, GA	$133,440
Chicago, IL	$129,600
Denver, CO	$145,600
Los Angeles, CA	$56,260
Minneapolis-St. Paul, MN	$138,070
New York, NY	$86,330
Phoenix, AZ	$67,760
San Francisco, CA	$108,800
Seattle, WA	$138,190

Average Earnings in Most Important Industries

Industry	Average Annual Earnings
Ambulatory Health Care Services	$103,140

POLICE AND DETECTIVES

- Average Earnings: $49,445
- Beginning Earnings: $29,092
- 25th Percentile: $37,652
- 75th Percentile: $62,371

Average Earnings in Major Metropolitan Areas

Metropolitan Area	Average Annual Earnings
Atlanta, GA	$40,567
Chicago, IL	$78,012
Dallas-Fort Worth, TX	$49,370
Denver, CO	$60,545
Los Angeles, CA	$67,842
Minneapolis-St. Paul, MN	$56,441
New York, NY	$60,500
Phoenix, AZ	$51,528
San Francisco, CA	$99,680
Seattle, WA	$63,984

Average Earnings in Most Important Industries

Industry	Average Annual Earnings
Federal, State, and Local Government	$49,616

POSTAL SERVICE WORKERS

- Average Earnings: $45,619
- Beginning Earnings: $30,244
- 25th Percentile: $38,492
- 75th Percentile: $51,183

Average Earnings in Major Metropolitan Areas

Metropolitan Area	Average Annual Earnings
Atlanta, GA	$44,615
Chicago, IL	$46,291
Dallas-Fort Worth, TX	$45,180
Denver, CO	$45,124
Los Angeles, CA	$47,283
Minneapolis-St. Paul, MN	$46,097
New York, NY	$45,679
Phoenix, AZ	$45,382
San Francisco, CA	$46,470
Seattle, WA	$45,340

Average Earnings in Most Important Industries

Industry	Average Annual Earnings
Postal Service	$45,619

POWER PLANT OPERATORS, DISTRIBUTORS, AND DISPATCHERS

- Average Earnings: $55,258
- Beginning Earnings: $36,613
- 25th Percentile: $45,687
- 75th Percentile: $65,625

Average Earnings in Major Metropolitan Areas

Metropolitan Area	Average Annual Earnings
Chicago, IL	$59,050
Dallas-Fort Worth, TX	$52,220
Los Angeles, CA	$59,970
Minneapolis-St. Paul, MN	$63,773
New York, NY	$65,307
San Francisco, CA	$60,420

Average Earnings in Most Important Industries

Industry	Average Annual Earnings
Management of Companies and Enterprises	$61,721
Utilities	$57,011
Federal, State, and Local Government	$49,174
Educational Services	$42,410
Hospitals	$39,700

PRECISION INSTRUMENT AND EQUIPMENT REPAIRERS

- Average Earnings: $39,003
- Beginning Earnings: $22,325
- 25th Percentile: $29,514
- 75th Percentile: $50,642

Average Earnings in Major Metropolitan Areas

Metropolitan Area	Average Annual Earnings
Atlanta, GA	$39,174
Chicago, IL	$37,435
Dallas-Fort Worth, TX	$45,070
Denver, CO	$51,030
Los Angeles, CA	$45,694
Minneapolis-St. Paul, MN	$42,747
New York, NY	$43,187
Seattle, WA	$46,299

Average Earnings in Most Important Industries

Industry	Average Annual Earnings
Hospitals	$41,730
Merchant Wholesalers, Durable Goods	$41,231
Repair and Maintenance	$37,748
Ambulatory Health Care Services	$34,206
Sporting Goods, Hobby, Book, and Music Stores	$28,000

PREPRESS TECHNICIANS AND WORKERS

- Average Earnings: $32,461
- Beginning Earnings: $19,525
- 25th Percentile: $24,843
- 75th Percentile: $41,558

Average Earnings in Major Metropolitan Areas

Metropolitan Area	Average Annual Earnings
Atlanta, GA	$34,495
Chicago, IL	$36,878
Dallas-Fort Worth, TX	$30,254
Denver, CO	$45,850
Los Angeles, CA	$36,223
Minneapolis-St. Paul, MN	$43,131
New York, NY	$38,728
Phoenix, AZ	$30,300
San Francisco, CA	$46,390
Seattle, WA	$38,412

Average Earnings in Most Important Industries

Industry	Average Annual Earnings
Paper Manufacturing	$33,910
Printing and Related Support Activities	$32,736
Publishing Industries (Except Internet)	$32,005
Professional, Scientific, and Technical Services	$30,457
Administrative and Support Services	$27,383

PRINTING MACHINE OPERATORS

- Average Earnings: $30,730
- Beginning Earnings: $18,450
- 25th Percentile: $23,050
- 75th Percentile: $40,230

Average Earnings in Major Metropolitan Areas

Metropolitan Area	Average Annual Earnings
Atlanta, GA	$32,950
Chicago, IL	$30,850
Dallas-Fort Worth, TX	$29,220
Denver, CO	$34,410
Los Angeles, CA	$29,720
Minneapolis-St. Paul, MN	$38,640
New York, NY	$33,300
Phoenix, AZ	$28,840
San Francisco, CA	$42,060
Seattle, WA	$34,300

Average Earnings in Most Important Industries

Industry	Average Annual Earnings
Printing and Related Support Activities	$31,920
Publishing Industries (Except Internet)	$35,120
Paper Manufacturing	$33,860
Plastics and Rubber Products Manufacturing	$29,900
Professional, Scientific, and Technical Services	$25,550

PRIVATE DETECTIVES AND INVESTIGATORS

- Average Earnings: $32,650
- Beginning Earnings: $19,230
- 25th Percentile: $24,030
- 75th Percentile: $44,290

Average Earnings in Major Metropolitan Areas

Metropolitan Area	Average Annual Earnings
Atlanta, GA	$28,950
Denver, CO	$39,330
Los Angeles, CA	$40,870
Minneapolis-St. Paul, MN	$29,360
Phoenix, AZ	$35,520
San Francisco, CA	$41,330
Seattle, WA	$38,970

Average Earnings in Most Important Industries

Industry	Average Annual Earnings
Credit Intermediation and Related Activities	$48,090
Professional, Scientific, and Technical Services	$43,990
Federal, State, and Local Government	$41,100
Insurance Carriers and Related Activities	$40,520
Administrative and Support Services	$30,910

PROBATION OFFICERS AND CORRECTIONAL TREATMENT SPECIALISTS

- Average Earnings: $40,210
- Beginning Earnings: $27,600
- 25th Percentile: $32,160
- 75th Percentile: $52,830

Average Earnings in Major Metropolitan Areas

Metropolitan Area	Average Annual Earnings
Atlanta, GA	$32,400
Dallas-Fort Worth, TX	$33,860
Denver, CO	$54,040
Minneapolis-St. Paul, MN	$56,390
San Francisco, CA	$72,730

Average Earnings in Most Important Industries

Industry	Average Annual Earnings
Federal, State, and Local Government	$40,620

PROCUREMENT CLERKS

- Average Earnings: $32,210
- Beginning Earnings: $20,500
- 25th Percentile: $25,510
- 75th Percentile: $39,290

Average Earnings in Major Metropolitan Areas

Metropolitan Area	Average Annual Earnings
Atlanta, GA	$31,390
Chicago, IL	$34,000
Dallas-Fort Worth, TX	$34,360
Denver, CO	$35,860
Los Angeles, CA	$32,980
Minneapolis-St. Paul, MN	$31,890
New York, NY	$33,970
Phoenix, AZ	$34,180
San Francisco, CA	$40,280
Seattle, WA	$34,720

Average Earnings in Most Important Industries

Industry	Average Annual Earnings
Federal, State, and Local Government	$37,150
Management of Companies and Enterprises	$31,780
Merchant Wholesalers, Nondurable Goods	$31,300
Educational Services	$30,940
Hospitals	$28,560

PRODUCTION, PLANNING, AND EXPEDITING CLERKS

- Average Earnings: $37,590
- Beginning Earnings: $22,860
- 25th Percentile: $28,740
- 75th Percentile: $47,700

Average Earnings in Major Metropolitan Areas

Metropolitan Area	Average Annual Earnings
Atlanta, GA	$38,440
Chicago, IL	$38,560
Dallas-Fort Worth, TX	$39,120
Denver, CO	$40,860
Los Angeles, CA	$38,800
Minneapolis-St. Paul, MN	$41,650
New York, NY	$42,160
Phoenix, AZ	$37,230
San Francisco, CA	$45,340
Seattle, WA	$41,310

Average Earnings in Most Important Industries

Industry	Average Annual Earnings
Transportation Equipment Manufacturing	$41,550
Computer and Electronic Product Manufacturing	$40,230
Professional, Scientific, and Technical Services	$38,830
Machinery Manufacturing	$38,210
Merchant Wholesalers, Durable Goods	$35,480

PROPERTY, REAL ESTATE, AND COMMUNITY ASSOCIATION MANAGERS

- Average Earnings: $41,900
- Beginning Earnings: $20,100
- 25th Percentile: $28,230
- 75th Percentile: $61,060

Average Earnings in Major Metropolitan Areas

Metropolitan Area	Average Annual Earnings
Atlanta, GA	$48,330
Chicago, IL	$52,370
Dallas-Fort Worth, TX	$34,660
Denver, CO	$52,720
Los Angeles, CA	$35,330
Minneapolis-St. Paul, MN	$44,110
New York, NY	$62,560
Phoenix, AZ	$42,240
San Francisco, CA	$44,390
Seattle, WA	$53,240

Average Earnings in Most Important Industries

Industry	Average Annual Earnings
Real Estate	$38,490

PSYCHOLOGISTS

- Average Earnings: $58,528
- Beginning Earnings: $34,133
- 25th Percentile: $44,411
- 75th Percentile: $76,080

Average Earnings in Major Metropolitan Areas

Metropolitan Area	Average Annual Earnings
Atlanta, GA	$62,627
Chicago, IL	$56,665
Dallas-Fort Worth, TX	$55,670
Denver, CO	$61,529
Los Angeles, CA	$71,110
Minneapolis-St. Paul, MN	$60,617
New York, NY	$74,374
Phoenix, AZ	$46,257
San Francisco, CA	$73,850
Seattle, WA	$55,370

Average Earnings in Most Important Industries

Industry	Average Annual Earnings
Federal, State, and Local Government	$64,433
Hospitals	$61,562
Ambulatory Health Care Services	$60,616
Educational Services	$57,704
Social Assistance	$45,900

PUBLIC RELATIONS SPECIALISTS

- Average Earnings: $45,020
- Beginning Earnings: $26,870
- 25th Percentile: $33,940
- 75th Percentile: $61,920

Average Earnings in Major Metropolitan Areas

Metropolitan Area	Average Annual Earnings
Atlanta, GA	$44,490
Chicago, IL	$46,930
Dallas-Fort Worth, TX	$50,540
Denver, CO	$44,980
Los Angeles, CA	$43,970
Minneapolis-St. Paul, MN	$45,720
New York, NY	$49,770
Phoenix, AZ	$39,490
San Francisco, CA	$52,570
Seattle, WA	$51,490

Average Earnings in Most Important Industries

Industry	Average Annual Earnings
Management of Companies and Enterprises	$51,890
Federal, State, and Local Government	$49,650
Professional, Scientific, and Technical Services	$48,820
Religious, Grantmaking, Civic, Professional, and Similar Organizations	$44,380
Educational Services	$41,600

PURCHASING MANAGERS, BUYERS, AND PURCHASING AGENTS

- Average Earnings: $51,182
- Beginning Earnings: $30,679
- 25th Percentile: $39,010
- 75th Percentile: $67,756

Average Earnings in Major Metropolitan Areas

Metropolitan Area	Average Annual Earnings
Atlanta, GA	$55,077
Chicago, IL	$51,273
Dallas-Fort Worth, TX	$54,799
Denver, CO	$51,956
Los Angeles, CA	$53,121
Minneapolis-St. Paul, MN	$58,456
New York, NY	$61,922
Phoenix, AZ	$47,110
San Francisco, CA	$60,658
Seattle, WA	$54,833

Average Earnings in Most Important Industries

Industry	Average Annual Earnings
Federal, State, and Local Government	$60,271
Professional, Scientific, and Technical Services	$59,970
Management of Companies and Enterprises	$59,350
Merchant Wholesalers, Nondurable Goods	$47,410
Merchant Wholesalers, Durable Goods	$46,683

RADIATION THERAPISTS

- Average Earnings: $62,340
- Beginning Earnings: $42,380
- 25th Percentile: $51,270
- 75th Percentile: $73,600

Average Earnings in Major Metropolitan Areas

Metropolitan Area	Average Annual Earnings
Seattle, WA	$78,180
Los Angeles, CA	$76,760
New York, NY	$76,030
Denver, CO	$69,570
Dallas-Fort Worth, TX	$59,920
Chicago, IL	$47,160

Average Earnings in Most Important Industries

Industry	Average Annual Earnings
Ambulatory Services	$66,220
Hospitals	$60,700

RADIO AND TELECOMMUNICATIONS EQUIPMENT INSTALLERS AND REPAIRERS

- Average Earnings: $50,238
- Beginning Earnings: $31,372
- 25th Percentile: $41,432
- 75th Percentile: $57,051

Average Earnings in Major Metropolitan Areas

Metropolitan Area	Average Annual Earnings
Atlanta, GA	$44,291
Chicago, IL	$57,186
Denver, CO	$51,530
Minneapolis-St. Paul, MN	$51,596
New York, NY	$62,110
Phoenix, AZ	$49,840
Seattle, WA	$50,760

Average Earnings in Most Important Industries

Industry	Average Annual Earnings
Telecommunications	$52,078
Professional, Scientific, and Technical Services	$51,100
Merchant Wholesalers, Durable Goods	$46,427
Specialty Trade Contractors	$39,850
Repair and Maintenance	$36,488

RADIOLOGIC TECHNOLOGISTS AND TECHNICIANS

- Average Earnings: $45,950
- Beginning Earnings: $31,290
- 25th Percentile: $38,250
- 75th Percentile: $55,100

Average Earnings in Major Metropolitan Areas

Metropolitan Area	Average Annual Earnings
Atlanta, GA	$47,130
Chicago, IL	$45,290
Dallas-Fort Worth, TX	$46,520
Denver, CO	$48,100
Los Angeles, CA	$51,210
Minneapolis-St. Paul, MN	$50,920
New York, NY	$57,350
Phoenix, AZ	$43,170
San Francisco, CA	$65,340
Seattle, WA	$55,280

Average Earnings in Most Important Industries

Industry	Average Annual Earnings
Hospitals	$46,290
Ambulatory Health Care Services	$45,070

RAIL TRANSPORTATION OCCUPATIONS

- Average Earnings: $51,383
- Beginning Earnings: $32,842
- 25th Percentile: $39,781
- 75th Percentile: $68,246

Average Earnings in Major Metropolitan Areas

Metropolitan Area	Average Annual Earnings
Atlanta, GA	$39,221
Chicago, IL	$32,810

Average Earnings in Most Important Industries

Industry	Average Annual Earnings
Rail Transportation	$52,978

REAL ESTATE BROKERS AND SALES AGENTS

- Average Earnings: $43,145
- Beginning Earnings: $20,543
- 25th Percentile: $28,104
- 75th Percentile: $71,661

Average Earnings in Major Metropolitan Areas

Metropolitan Area	Average Annual Earnings
Atlanta, GA	$31,867
Chicago, IL	$42,650
Dallas-Fort Worth, TX	$43,510
Denver, CO	$34,517
Los Angeles, CA	$59,166
Minneapolis-St. Paul, MN	$46,842
New York, NY	$53,274
Phoenix, AZ	$45,241
San Francisco, CA	$87,203
Seattle, WA	$53,684

Average Earnings in Most Important Industries

Industry	Average Annual Earnings
Real Estate	$41,681

RECEPTIONISTS AND INFORMATION CLERKS

- Average Earnings: $22,150
- Beginning Earnings: $15,200
- 25th Percentile: $18,330
- 75th Percentile: $27,200

Average Earnings in Major Metropolitan Areas

Metropolitan Area	Average Annual Earnings
Atlanta, GA	$24,370
Chicago, IL	$23,880
Dallas-Fort Worth, TX	$23,860
Denver, CO	$25,970
Los Angeles, CA	$23,770
Minneapolis-St. Paul, MN	$25,400
New York, NY	$26,170
Phoenix, AZ	$23,030
San Francisco, CA	$27,950
Seattle, WA	$24,970

Average Earnings in Most Important Industries

Industry	Average Annual Earnings
Ambulatory Health Care Services	$23,220
Professional, Scientific, and Technical Services	$23,090
Educational Services	$22,520
Administrative and Support Services	$21,770
Personal and Laundry Services	$17,330

RECREATION WORKERS

- Average Earnings: $20,110
- Beginning Earnings: $13,810
- 25th Percentile: $16,170
- 75th Percentile: $26,330

Average Earnings in Major Metropolitan Areas

Metropolitan Area	Average Annual Earnings
Atlanta, GA	$19,310
Chicago, IL	$19,700
Dallas-Fort Worth, TX	$19,320
Denver, CO	$22,960
Los Angeles, CA	$20,800
Minneapolis-St. Paul, MN	$22,030
New York, NY	$21,570
Phoenix, AZ	$23,250
San Francisco, CA	$24,080

Average Earnings in Most Important Industries

Industry	Average Annual Earnings
Nursing and Residential Care Facilities	$21,250
Federal, State, and Local Government	$20,570
Social Assistance	$20,330
Amusement, Gambling, and Recreation Industries	$18,480
Religious, Grantmaking, Civic, Professional, and Similar Organizations	$17,480

RECREATIONAL THERAPISTS

- Average Earnings: $33,480
- Beginning Earnings: $20,140
- 25th Percentile: $25,970
- 75th Percentile: $43,240

Average Earnings in Major Metropolitan Areas

Metropolitan Area	Average Annual Earnings
Atlanta, GA	$33,550
Chicago, IL	$31,400
Dallas-Fort Worth, TX	$35,560
Denver, CO	$40,930
Los Angeles, CA	$42,940
Minneapolis-St. Paul, MN	$37,270
New York, NY	$42,490
Phoenix, AZ	$33,370
San Francisco, CA	$50,050
Seattle, WA	$45,270

Average Earnings in Most Important Industries

Industry	Average Annual Earnings
Federal, State, and Local Government	$39,530
Hospitals	$37,970
Ambulatory Health Care Services	$33,030
Nursing and Residential Care Facilities	$29,280
Social Assistance	$25,380

REGISTERED NURSES

- Average Earnings: $54,670
- Beginning Earnings: $38,660
- 25th Percentile: $45,710
- 75th Percentile: $66,650

Average Earnings in Major Metropolitan Areas

Metropolitan Area	Average Annual Earnings
Atlanta, GA	$52,970
Chicago, IL	$54,340
Dallas-Fort Worth, TX	$54,240
Denver, CO	$59,240
Los Angeles, CA	$67,430
Minneapolis-St. Paul, MN	$61,680
New York, NY	$67,390
Phoenix, AZ	$57,000
San Francisco, CA	$80,470
Seattle, WA	$66,400

Average Earnings in Most Important Industries

Industry	Average Annual Earnings
Federal, State, and Local Government	$56,470
Hospitals	$55,740
Ambulatory Health Care Services	$52,090
Nursing and Residential Care Facilities	$50,020
Educational Services	$46,650

RESERVATION AND TRANSPORTATION TICKET AGENTS AND TRAVEL CLERKS

- Average Earnings: $28,120
- Beginning Earnings: $17,730
- 25th Percentile: $21,560
- 75th Percentile: $38,980

Average Earnings in Major Metropolitan Areas

Metropolitan Area	Average Annual Earnings
Denver, CO	$28,810
Los Angeles, CA	$27,920
New York, NY	$32,160
Phoenix, AZ	$21,190
San Francisco, CA	$28,640
Seattle, WA	$29,990

Average Earnings in Most Important Industries

Industry	Average Annual Earnings
Air Transportation	$32,650
Accommodation	$22,420
Administrative and Support Services	$22,290
Support Activities for Transportation	$22,250
Transit and Ground Passenger Transportation	$21,050

RESPIRATORY THERAPISTS

- Average Earnings: $43,836
- Beginning Earnings: $32,177
- 25th Percentile: $37,616
- 75th Percentile: $51,835

Average Earnings in Major Metropolitan Areas

Metropolitan Area	Average Annual Earnings
Atlanta, GA	$43,286
Chicago, IL	$43,960
Dallas-Fort Worth, TX	$42,245
Denver, CO	$45,867
Los Angeles, CA	$53,380
Minneapolis-St. Paul, MN	$50,381
New York, NY	$55,404
Phoenix, AZ	$40,678
San Francisco, CA	$59,620
Seattle, WA	$52,652

Average Earnings in Most Important Industries

Industry	Average Annual Earnings
Hospitals	$43,782

RETAIL SALESPERSONS

- Average Earnings: $19,140
- Beginning Earnings: $13,590
- 25th Percentile: $15,690
- 75th Percentile: $25,890

Average Earnings in Major Metropolitan Areas

Metropolitan Area	Average Annual Earnings
Atlanta, GA	$19,550
Chicago, IL	$19,520
Dallas-Fort Worth, TX	$19,020
Denver, CO	$20,870
Los Angeles, CA	$20,190
Minneapolis-St. Paul, MN	$19,410
New York, NY	$19,900
Phoenix, AZ	$20,810
San Francisco, CA	$21,540
Seattle, WA	$23,340

Average Earnings in Most Important Industries

Industry	Average Annual Earnings
Motor Vehicle and Parts Dealers	$34,190
Building Material and Garden Equipment and Supplies Dealers	$22,540
General Merchandise Stores	$17,620
Miscellaneous Store Retailers	$17,440
Clothing and Clothing Accessories Stores	$17,290

ROOFERS

- Average Earnings: $31,230
- Beginning Earnings: $19,580
- 25th Percentile: $24,230
- 75th Percentile: $41,110

Average Earnings in Major Metropolitan Areas

Metropolitan Area	Average Annual Earnings
Atlanta, GA	$29,150
Chicago, IL	$45,300
Dallas-Fort Worth, TX	$25,410
Denver, CO	$27,900
Los Angeles, CA	$39,280
Minneapolis-St. Paul, MN	$52,550
New York, NY	$36,150
Phoenix, AZ	$28,060
San Francisco, CA	$38,640
Seattle, WA	$43,570

Average Earnings in Most Important Industries

Industry	Average Annual Earnings
Specialty Trade Contractors	$31,240

SALES ENGINEERS

- Average Earnings: $74,200
- Beginning Earnings: $43,730
- 25th Percentile: $56,370
- 75th Percentile: $95,420

Average Earnings in Major Metropolitan Areas

Metropolitan Area	Average Annual Earnings
Atlanta, GA	$76,170
Chicago, IL	$67,660
Dallas-Fort Worth, TX	$85,300
Denver, CO	$71,290
Los Angeles, CA	$79,810
Minneapolis-St. Paul, MN	$71,260
New York, NY	$81,150
Phoenix, AZ	$62,580
San Francisco, CA	$98,230
Seattle, WA	$82,700

Average Earnings in Most Important Industries

Industry	Average Annual Earnings
Professional, Scientific, and Technical Services	$85,630
Wholesale Electronic Markets and Agents and Brokers	$78,920
Computer and Electronic Product Manufacturing	$77,070
Merchant Wholesalers, Durable Goods	$68,710
Machinery Manufacturing	$64,940

SALES REPRESENTATIVES, WHOLESALE AND MANUFACTURING

- Average Earnings: $50,178
- Beginning Earnings: $26,306
- 25th Percentile: $35,825
- 75th Percentile: $71,953

Average Earnings in Major Metropolitan Areas

Metropolitan Area	Average Annual Earnings
Atlanta, GA	$53,721
Chicago, IL	$54,142
Dallas-Fort Worth, TX	$53,979
Denver, CO	$52,696
Los Angeles, CA	$50,082
Minneapolis-St. Paul, MN	$56,232
New York, NY	$59,075
Phoenix, AZ	$43,115
San Francisco, CA	$57,067
Seattle, WA	$55,273

Average Earnings in Most Important Industries

Industry	Average Annual Earnings
Professional, Scientific, and Technical Services	$62,756
Wholesale Electronic Markets and Agents and Brokers	$54,187
Specialty Trade Contractors	$48,957
Merchant Wholesalers, Durable Goods	$48,503
Merchant Wholesalers, Nondurable Goods	$48,338

SALES WORKER SUPERVISORS

- Average Earnings: $39,056
- Beginning Earnings: $23,058
- 25th Percentile: $29,864
- 75th Percentile: $53,145

Average Earnings in Major Metropolitan Areas

Metropolitan Area	Average Annual Earnings
Atlanta, GA	$38,245
Chicago, IL	$45,074
Dallas-Fort Worth, TX	$42,032
Denver, CO	$45,125
Los Angeles, CA	$40,665
Minneapolis-St. Paul, MN	$48,777
New York, NY	$56,830
Phoenix, AZ	$38,254
San Francisco, CA	$43,685
Seattle, WA	$50,156

Average Earnings in Most Important Industries

Industry	Average Annual Earnings
Motor Vehicle and Parts Dealers	$51,201
Building Material and Garden Equipment and Supplies Dealers	$35,386
Clothing and Clothing Accessories Stores	$32,180
Food and Beverage Stores	$31,888
General Merchandise Stores	$29,020

SCIENCE TECHNICIANS

- Average Earnings: $36,261
- Beginning Earnings: $22,769
- 25th Percentile: $28,574
- 75th Percentile: $46,385

Average Earnings in Major Metropolitan Areas

Metropolitan Area	Average Annual Earnings
Atlanta, GA	$32,830
Chicago, IL	$34,312
Dallas-Fort Worth, TX	$39,160
Denver, CO	$41,404
Los Angeles, CA	$38,474
Minneapolis-St. Paul, MN	$36,260
New York, NY	$38,818
Phoenix, AZ	$38,149
San Francisco, CA	$42,920
Seattle, WA	$41,410

Average Earnings in Most Important Industries

Industry	Average Annual Earnings
Chemical Manufacturing	$39,844
Professional, Scientific, and Technical Services	$35,273
Educational Services	$33,188
Federal, State, and Local Government	$33,142
Food Manufacturing	$32,770

SECRETARIES AND ADMINISTRATIVE ASSISTANTS

- Average Earnings: $30,996
- Beginning Earnings: $20,413
- 25th Percentile: $24,936
- 75th Percentile: $38,609

Average Earnings in Major Metropolitan Areas

Metropolitan Area	Average Annual Earnings
Atlanta, GA	$31,984
Chicago, IL	$32,949
Dallas-Fort Worth, TX	$31,500
Denver, CO	$37,366
Los Angeles, CA	$37,725
Minneapolis-St. Paul, MN	$37,927
New York, NY	$37,087
Phoenix, AZ	$30,308
San Francisco, CA	$42,877
Seattle, WA	$36,875

Average Earnings in Most Important Industries

Industry	Average Annual Earnings
Professional, Scientific, and Technical Services	$34,675
Federal, State, and Local Government	$33,739
Educational Services	$29,832
Administrative and Support Services	$29,144
Ambulatory Health Care Services	$28,369

SECURITIES, COMMODITIES, AND FINANCIAL SERVICES SALES AGENTS

- Average Earnings: $67,130
- Beginning Earnings: $30,130
- 25th Percentile: $42,330
- 75th Percentile: $123,910

Average Earnings in Major Metropolitan Areas

Metropolitan Area	Average Annual Earnings
Atlanta, GA	$52,940
Chicago, IL	$57,910
Dallas-Fort Worth, TX	$58,380
Denver, CO	$69,960
Minneapolis-St. Paul, MN	$69,160
New York, NY	$97,440
Phoenix, AZ	$52,860
San Francisco, CA	$94,810
Seattle, WA	$56,010

Average Earnings in Most Important Industries

Industry	Average Annual Earnings
Securities, Commodity Contracts, and Other Financial Investments and Related Activities	$79,450
Professional, Scientific, and Technical Services	$76,530
Management of Companies and Enterprises	$66,430
Credit Intermediation and Related Activities	$50,340
Insurance Carriers and Related Activities	$49,320

SECURITY GUARDS AND GAMING SURVEILLANCE OFFICERS

- Average Earnings: $22,030
- Beginning Earnings: $14,929
- 25th Percentile: $17,823
- 75th Percentile: $27,981

Average Earnings in Major Metropolitan Areas

Metropolitan Area	Average Annual Earnings
Atlanta, GA	$21,418
Chicago, IL	$22,130
Dallas-Fort Worth, TX	$22,311
Denver, CO	$25,759
Los Angeles, CA	$21,612
Minneapolis-St. Paul, MN	$25,739
New York, NY	$22,583
Phoenix, AZ	$21,196
San Francisco, CA	$26,443
Seattle, WA	$25,526

Average Earnings in Most Important Industries

Industry	Average Annual Earnings
Federal, State, and Local Government	$30,331
Hospitals	$25,829
Educational Services	$24,276
Accommodation	$21,983
Administrative and Support Services	$19,656

SEMICONDUCTOR PROCESSORS

- Average Earnings: $31,030
- Beginning Earnings: $20,790
- 25th Percentile: $25,290
- 75th Percentile: $37,780

Average Earnings in Major Metropolitan Areas

Metropolitan Area	Average Annual Earnings
Los Angeles, CA	$31,970
Minneapolis-St. Paul, MN	$32,050
New York, NY	$31,040
San Francisco, CA	$31,010

Average Earnings in Most Important Industries

Industry	Average Annual Earnings
Computer and Electronic Product Manufacturing	$31,020

SHEET METAL WORKERS

- Average Earnings: $36,390
- Beginning Earnings: $20,760
- 25th Percentile: $26,840
- 75th Percentile: $50,650

Average Earnings in Major Metropolitan Areas

Metropolitan Area	Average Annual Earnings
Atlanta, GA	$32,720
Chicago, IL	$63,090
Dallas-Fort Worth, TX	$26,380
Los Angeles, CA	$42,140
Minneapolis-St. Paul, MN	$52,620
New York, NY	$61,920
Phoenix, AZ	$33,530
San Francisco, CA	$54,380
Seattle, WA	$44,940

Average Earnings in Most Important Industries

Industry	Average Annual Earnings
Federal, State, and Local Government	$46,140
Transportation Equipment Manufacturing	$40,100
Specialty Trade Contractors	$36,610
Fabricated Metal Product Manufacturing	$33,320
Machinery Manufacturing	$30,750

SHIPPING, RECEIVING, AND TRAFFIC CLERKS

- Average Earnings: $25,180
- Beginning Earnings: $16,520
- 25th Percentile: $20,020
- 75th Percentile: $31,900

Average Earnings in Major Metropolitan Areas

Metropolitan Area	Average Annual Earnings
Atlanta, GA	$26,220
Chicago, IL	$26,370
Dallas-Fort Worth, TX	$23,630
Denver, CO	$26,870
Los Angeles, CA	$23,920
Minneapolis-St. Paul, MN	$29,230
New York, NY	$26,110
San Francisco, CA	$29,330
Seattle, WA	$28,570

Average Earnings in Most Important Industries

Industry	Average Annual Earnings
Warehousing and Storage	$27,110
Merchant Wholesalers, Nondurable Goods	$25,560
Merchant Wholesalers, Durable Goods	$25,390
Administrative and Support Services	$20,820
General Merchandise Stores	$19,500

SMALL ENGINE MECHANICS

- Average Earnings: $28,954
- Beginning Earnings: $18,197
- 25th Percentile: $22,834
- 75th Percentile: $36,559

Average Earnings in Major Metropolitan Areas

Metropolitan Area	Average Annual Earnings
Atlanta, GA	$32,925
Chicago, IL	$31,655
Dallas-Fort Worth, TX	$31,053
Denver, CO	$37,550
Los Angeles, CA	$33,099
Minneapolis-St. Paul, MN	$33,249
New York, NY	$31,489
Phoenix, AZ	$26,614
San Francisco, CA	$39,355
Seattle, WA	$37,654

Average Earnings in Most Important Industries

Industry	Average Annual Earnings
Amusement, Gambling, and Recreation Industries	$33,789
Motor Vehicle and Parts Dealers	$30,182
Repair and Maintenance	$29,450
Merchant Wholesalers, Durable Goods	$27,132
Rental and Leasing Services	$26,789

SOCIAL AND HUMAN SERVICE ASSISTANTS

- Average Earnings: $25,030
- Beginning Earnings: $15,830
- 25th Percentile: $19,850
- 75th Percentile: $31,830

Average Earnings in Major Metropolitan Areas

Metropolitan Area	Average Annual Earnings
Atlanta, GA	$25,930
Chicago, IL	$23,790
Dallas-Fort Worth, TX	$19,340
Denver, CO	$29,740
Los Angeles, CA	$28,540
Minneapolis-St. Paul, MN	$26,840
New York, NY	$27,400
Phoenix, AZ	$28,290
San Francisco, CA	$29,730
Seattle, WA	$23,300

Average Earnings in Most Important Industries

Industry	Average Annual Earnings
Federal, State, and Local Government	$28,960
Ambulatory Health Care Services	$24,420
Religious, Grantmaking, Civic, Professional, and Similar Organizations	$24,610
Social Assistance	$23,590
Nursing and Residential Care Facilities	$22,280

SOCIAL SCIENTISTS, OTHER

- Average Earnings: $61,450
- Beginning Earnings: $35,109
- 25th Percentile: $45,955
- 75th Percentile: $80,054

Average Earnings in Major Metropolitan Areas

Metropolitan Area	Average Annual Earnings
Atlanta, GA	$65,957
Chicago, IL	$55,970
Dallas-Fort Worth, TX	$67,300
Denver, CO	$66,770
Los Angeles, CA	$61,050
Minneapolis-St. Paul, MN	$59,131
New York, NY	$61,237
Phoenix, AZ	$49,849
San Francisco, CA	$64,401
Seattle, WA	$56,489

Average Earnings in Most Important Industries

Industry	Average Annual Earnings
Federal, State, and Local Government	$67,263
Religious, Grantmaking, Civic, Professional, and Similar Organizations	$62,821
Professional, Scientific, and Technical Services	$53,148
Educational Services	$48,657
Ambulatory Health Care Services	$47,910

SOCIAL WORKERS

- Average Earnings: $36,982
- Beginning Earnings: $23,866
- 25th Percentile: $29,423
- 75th Percentile: $47,764

Average Earnings in Major Metropolitan Areas

Metropolitan Area	Average Annual Earnings
Atlanta, GA	$35,784
Chicago, IL	$40,129
Dallas-Fort Worth, TX	$36,072
Denver, CO	$40,000
Los Angeles, CA	$44,881
Minneapolis-St. Paul, MN	$46,251
New York, NY	$44,432
Phoenix, AZ	$34,769
San Francisco, CA	$43,240
Seattle, WA	$41,971

Average Earnings in Most Important Industries

Industry	Average Annual Earnings
Hospitals	$43,829
Federal, State, and Local Government	$39,714
Ambulatory Health Care Services	$37,318
Nursing and Residential Care Facilities	$32,395
Social Assistance	$31,634

SPEECH-LANGUAGE PATHOLOGISTS

- Average Earnings: $54,880
- Beginning Earnings: $36,380
- 25th Percentile: $44,080
- 75th Percentile: $69,060

Average Earnings in Major Metropolitan Areas

Metropolitan Area	Average Annual Earnings
Atlanta, GA	$54,460
Chicago, IL	$56,000
Dallas-Fort Worth, TX	$48,150
Denver, CO	$56,380
Los Angeles, CA	$66,910
Minneapolis-St. Paul, MN	$52,530
New York, NY	$67,450
Phoenix, AZ	$43,790
San Francisco, CA	$70,380
Seattle, WA	$55,260

Average Earnings in Most Important Industries

Industry	Average Annual Earnings
Nursing and Residential Care Facilities	$65,800
Ambulatory Health Care Services	$60,070
Hospitals	$58,190
Social Assistance	$54,540
Educational Services	$50,760

STATIONARY ENGINEERS AND BOILER OPERATORS

- Average Earnings: $44,600
- Beginning Earnings: $27,850
- 25th Percentile: $35,330
- 75th Percentile: $55,560

Average Earnings in Major Metropolitan Areas

Metropolitan Area	Average Annual Earnings
Chicago, IL	$54,040
Dallas-Fort Worth, TX	$48,900
Denver, CO	$44,600
Los Angeles, CA	$53,260
Minneapolis-St. Paul, MN	$49,170
New York, NY	$54,590
Phoenix, AZ	$39,750
Seattle, WA	$49,260

Average Earnings in Most Important Industries

Industry	Average Annual Earnings
Utilities	$50,200
Federal, State, and Local Government	$47,270
Paper Manufacturing	$45,370
Hospitals	$45,700
Educational Services	$41,420

STATISTICIANS

- Average Earnings: $62,450
- Beginning Earnings: $35,110
- 25th Percentile: $45,260
- 75th Percentile: $83,830

Average Earnings in Major Metropolitan Areas

Metropolitan Area	Average Annual Earnings
Atlanta, GA	$49,320
Chicago, IL	$60,730
Dallas-Fort Worth, TX	$49,120
Denver, CO	$62,890
Los Angeles, CA	$69,990
Minneapolis-St. Paul, MN	$61,710
New York, NY	$66,880
Phoenix, AZ	$61,020
San Francisco, CA	$81,050
Seattle, WA	$55,910

Average Earnings in Most Important Industries

Industry	Average Annual Earnings
Chemical Manufacturing	$76,760
Federal, State, and Local Government	$68,140
Professional, Scientific, and Technical Services	$67,400
Insurance Carriers and Related Activities	$54,540
Educational Services	$51,140

STOCK CLERKS AND ORDER FILLERS

- Average Earnings: $20,100
- Beginning Earnings: $14,180
- 25th Percentile: $16,320
- 75th Percentile: $26,030

Average Earnings in Major Metropolitan Areas

Metropolitan Area	Average Annual Earnings
Atlanta, GA	$21,360
Chicago, IL	$19,570
Dallas-Fort Worth, TX	$21,250
Denver, CO	$23,110
Los Angeles, CA	$20,600
Minneapolis-St. Paul, MN	$22,610
New York, NY	$19,540
Phoenix, AZ	$19,110
San Francisco, CA	$23,410
Seattle, WA	$24,280

Average Earnings in Most Important Industries

Industry	Average Annual Earnings
Warehousing and Storage	$26,670
Merchant Wholesalers, Durable Goods	$23,350
Merchant Wholesalers, Nondurable Goods	$22,530
Food and Beverage Stores	$18,390
General Merchandise Stores	$18,370

STRUCTURAL AND REINFORCING IRON AND METAL WORKERS

- Average Earnings: $38,849
- Beginning Earnings: $21,829
- 25th Percentile: $28,485
- 75th Percentile: $55,163

Average Earnings in Major Metropolitan Areas

Metropolitan Area	Average Annual Earnings
Atlanta, GA	$31,050
Chicago, IL	$65,600
Dallas-Fort Worth, TX	$27,516
Denver, CO	$39,180
Los Angeles, CA	$50,060
Minneapolis-St. Paul, MN	$57,360
New York, NY	$71,510
Phoenix, AZ	$35,740
San Francisco, CA	$63,200
Seattle, WA	$52,170

Average Earnings in Most Important Industries

Industry	Average Annual Earnings
Fabricated Metal Product Manufacturing	$41,353
Specialty Trade Contractors	$39,998
Heavy and Civil Engineering Construction	$38,781
Construction of Buildings	$35,898
Administrative and Support Services	$32,940

SURGICAL TECHNOLOGISTS

- Average Earnings: $34,830
- Beginning Earnings: $24,530
- 25th Percentile: $29,330
- 75th Percentile: $42,010

Average Earnings in Major Metropolitan Areas

Metropolitan Area	Average Annual Earnings
Atlanta, GA	$33,210
Chicago, IL	$37,460
Dallas-Fort Worth, TX	$35,900
Denver, CO	$36,370
Los Angeles, CA	$41,220
Minneapolis-St. Paul, MN	$43,070
New York, NY	$37,140
Phoenix, AZ	$38,960
San Francisco, CA	$48,970
Seattle, WA	$43,180

Average Earnings in Most Important Industries

Industry	Average Annual Earnings
Hospitals	$34,350

SURVEYORS, CARTOGRAPHERS, PHOTOGRAMMETRISTS, AND SURVEYING TECHNICIANS

- Average Earnings: $38,871
- Beginning Earnings: $22,809
- 25th Percentile: $29,313
- 75th Percentile: $51,133

Average Earnings in Major Metropolitan Areas

Metropolitan Area	Average Annual Earnings
Atlanta, GA	$36,766
Chicago, IL	$45,092
Dallas-Fort Worth, TX	$37,558
Denver, CO	$49,431
Los Angeles, CA	$63,766
Minneapolis-St. Paul, MN	$46,768
New York, NY	$46,459
Phoenix, AZ	$39,049
San Francisco, CA	$63,137
Seattle, WA	$50,186

Average Earnings in Most Important Industries

Industry	Average Annual Earnings
Utilities	$44,773
Federal, State, and Local Government	$43,711
Heavy and Civil Engineering Construction	$43,051
Professional, Scientific, and Technical Services	$37,488
Administrative and Support Services	$32,425

TAX EXAMINERS, COLLECTORS, AND REVENUE AGENTS

- Average Earnings: $44,210
- Beginning Earnings: $25,950
- 25th Percentile: $33,630
- 75th Percentile: $63,440

Average Earnings in Major Metropolitan Areas

Metropolitan Area	Average Annual Earnings
Atlanta, GA	$41,120
Dallas-Fort Worth, TX	$65,510
Denver, CO	$55,220
Los Angeles, CA	$67,430
Minneapolis-St. Paul, MN	$54,210
New York, NY	$55,230
Phoenix, AZ	$56,220
San Francisco, CA	$68,100

Average Earnings in Most Important Industries

Industry	Average Annual Earnings
Federal, State, and Local Government	$44,210

TAXI DRIVERS AND CHAUFFEURS

- Average Earnings: $19,980
- Beginning Earnings: $13,900
- 25th Percentile: $16,250
- 75th Percentile: $24,940

Average Earnings in Major Metropolitan Areas

Metropolitan Area	Average Annual Earnings
Atlanta, GA	$23,110
Chicago, IL	$20,490
Dallas-Fort Worth, TX	$19,610
Denver, CO	$21,930
Los Angeles, CA	$20,280
New York, NY	$25,460
Phoenix, AZ	$20,460
San Francisco, CA	$23,510
Seattle, WA	$25,040

Average Earnings in Most Important Industries

Industry	Average Annual Earnings
Transit and Ground Passenger Transportation	$20,660
Nursing and Residential Care Facilities	$20,490
Personal and Laundry Services	$18,710
Social Assistance	$18,330
Motor Vehicle and Parts Dealers	$17,870

TEACHER ASSISTANTS

- Average Earnings: $20,090
- Beginning Earnings: $13,380
- 25th Percentile: $15,910
- 75th Percentile: $25,300

Average Earnings in Major Metropolitan Areas

Metropolitan Area	Average Annual Earnings
Atlanta, GA	$16,190
Chicago, IL	$19,600
Dallas-Fort Worth, TX	$17,240
Denver, CO	$23,810
Los Angeles, CA	$26,550
Minneapolis-St. Paul, MN	$21,470
New York, NY	$22,400
Phoenix, AZ	$19,260
San Francisco, CA	$28,060
Seattle, WA	$25,950

Average Earnings in Most Important Industries

Industry	Average Annual Earnings
Nursing and Residential Care Facilities	$22,020
Ambulatory Health Care Services	$20,600
Educational Services	$20,290
Religious, Grantmaking, Civic, Professional, and Similar Organizations	$18,170
Social Assistance	$17,770

TEACHERS—ADULT LITERACY AND REMEDIAL EDUCATION

- Average Earnings: $41,270
- Beginning Earnings: $23,420
- 25th Percentile: $30,760
- 75th Percentile: $54,350

Average Earnings in Major Metropolitan Areas

Metropolitan Area	Average Annual Earnings
Atlanta, GA	$41,020
Chicago, IL	$41,900
Dallas-Fort Worth, TX	$37,980
Denver, CO	$28,410
Los Angeles, CA	$72,480
Minneapolis-St. Paul, MN	$45,620
New York, NY	$51,390
Phoenix, AZ	$32,390
San Francisco, CA	$48,560
Seattle, WA	$41,430

Average Earnings in Most Important Industries

Industry	Average Annual Earnings
Educational Services	$42,980
Federal, State, and Local Government	$41,630
Nursing and Residential Care Facilities	$36,500
Social Assistance	$32,640
Administrative and Support Services	$31,110

TEACHERS— POSTSECONDARY

- Average Earnings: $41,810
- Beginning Earnings: $28,092
- 25th Percentile: $33,641
- 75th Percentile: $76,005

Average Earnings in Major Metropolitan Areas

Metropolitan Area	Average Annual Earnings
Atlanta, GA	$61,610
Chicago, IL	$58,121
Dallas-Fort Worth, TX	$56,857
Denver, CO	$53,780
Los Angeles, CA	$69,043
Minneapolis-St. Paul, MN	$55,598
New York, NY	$69,617
Phoenix, AZ	$44,165
San Francisco, CA	$72,634
Seattle, WA	$55,040

Average Earnings in Most Important Industries

Industry	Average Annual Earnings
Educational Services	$61,135

TEACHERS—PRESCHOOL, KINDERGARTEN, ELEMENTARY, MIDDLE, AND SECONDARY

- Average Earnings: $42,642
- Beginning Earnings: $28,454
- 25th Percentile: $34,388
- 75th Percentile: $54,416

Average Earnings in Major Metropolitan Areas

Metropolitan Area	Average Annual Earnings
Atlanta, GA	$39,598
Chicago, IL	$48,737
Dallas-Fort Worth, TX	$41,086
Denver, CO	$43,897
Los Angeles, CA	$50,470
Minneapolis-St. Paul, MN	$42,381
New York, NY	$62,789
Phoenix, AZ	$32,382
San Francisco, CA	$51,107
Seattle, WA	$42,869

Average Earnings in Most Important Industries

Industry	Average Annual Earnings
Educational Services	$44,571

TEACHERS—SELF-ENRICHMENT EDUCATION

- Average Earnings: $32,360
- Beginning Earnings: $17,140
- 25th Percentile: $22,590
- 75th Percentile: $45,380

Average Earnings in Major Metropolitan Areas

Metropolitan Area	Average Annual Earnings
Atlanta, GA	$29,550
Chicago, IL	$43,190
Dallas-Fort Worth, TX	$31,010
Denver, CO	$35,390
Los Angeles, CA	$32,150
Minneapolis-St. Paul, MN	$34,510
New York, NY	$39,870
Phoenix, AZ	$22,990
San Francisco, CA	$38,480
Seattle, WA	$35,530

Average Earnings in Most Important Industries

Industry	Average Annual Earnings
Educational Services	$34,310
Religious, Grantmaking, Civic, Professional, and Similar Organizations	$29,840
Amusement, Gambling, and Recreation Industries	$28,240
Social Assistance	$27,660
Sporting Goods, Hobby, Book, and Music Stores	$20,680

TEACHERS—SPECIAL EDUCATION

- Average Earnings: $45,484
- Beginning Earnings: $30,878
- 25th Percentile: $36,908
- 75th Percentile: $58,419

Average Earnings in Major Metropolitan Areas

Metropolitan Area	Average Annual Earnings
Atlanta, GA	$46,928
Chicago, IL	$48,259
Dallas-Fort Worth, TX	$43,797
Denver, CO	$48,658
Los Angeles, CA	$57,628
Minneapolis-St. Paul, MN	$48,860
New York, NY	$60,130
Phoenix, AZ	$37,367
San Francisco, CA	$56,651
Seattle, WA	$44,070

Average Earnings in Most Important Industries

Industry	Average Annual Earnings
Educational Services	$45,733

TELEVISION, VIDEO, AND MOTION PICTURE CAMERA OPERATORS AND EDITORS

- Average Earnings: $43,753
- Beginning Earnings: $19,591
- 25th Percentile: $28,745
- 75th Percentile: $63,747

Average Earnings in Major Metropolitan Areas

Metropolitan Area	Average Annual Earnings
Atlanta, GA	$27,933
Chicago, IL	$49,837
Dallas-Fort Worth, TX	$43,573
Denver, CO	$47,143
Los Angeles, CA	$64,830
Minneapolis-St. Paul, MN	$51,832
New York, NY	$49,476
Phoenix, AZ	$34,508
Seattle, WA	$40,960

Average Earnings in Most Important Industries

Industry	Average Annual Earnings
Motion Picture and Sound Recording Industries	$49,589
Federal, State, and Local Government	$48,985
Performing Arts, Spectator Sports, and Related Industries	$41,480
Professional, Scientific, and Technical Services	$39,016
Broadcasting (Except Internet)	$36,533

TELLERS

- Average Earnings: $21,300
- Beginning Earnings: $16,270
- 25th Percentile: $18,750
- 75th Percentile: $25,080

Average Earnings in Major Metropolitan Areas

Metropolitan Area	Average Annual Earnings
Atlanta, GA	$23,160
Chicago, IL	$20,860
Dallas-Fort Worth, TX	$21,140
Denver, CO	$24,770
Los Angeles, CA	$23,300
Minneapolis-St. Paul, MN	$22,120
New York, NY	$21,680
Phoenix, AZ	$21,560
San Francisco, CA	$25,620
Seattle, WA	$22,940

Average Earnings in Most Important Industries

Industry	Average Annual Earnings
Credit Intermediation and Related Activities	$21,280

TEXTILE, APPAREL, AND FURNISHINGS OCCUPATIONS

- Average Earnings: $19,985
- Beginning Earnings: $14,518
- 25th Percentile: $16,799
- 75th Percentile: $24,450

Average Earnings in Major Metropolitan Areas

Metropolitan Area	Average Annual Earnings
Atlanta, GA	$20,116
Chicago, IL	$19,711
Dallas-Fort Worth, TX	$18,686
Denver, CO	$20,535
Los Angeles, CA	$18,325
Minneapolis-St. Paul, MN	$25,389
New York, NY	$20,217
Phoenix, AZ	$17,798
San Francisco, CA	$20,634
Seattle, WA	$23,599

Average Earnings in Most Important Industries

Industry	Average Annual Earnings
Furniture and Related Product Manufacturing	$24,693
Textile Mills	$22,997
Textile Product Mills	$21,589
Apparel Manufacturing	$18,395
Personal and Laundry Services	$17,273

TOOL AND DIE MAKERS

- Average Earnings: $43,580
- Beginning Earnings: $28,500
- 25th Percentile: $35,660
- 75th Percentile: $54,930

Average Earnings in Major Metropolitan Areas

Metropolitan Area	Average Annual Earnings
Atlanta, GA	$41,090
Chicago, IL	$46,080
Dallas-Fort Worth, TX	$40,230
Denver, CO	$44,890
Los Angeles, CA	$45,280
Minneapolis-St. Paul, MN	$47,600
New York, NY	$45,020
Phoenix, AZ	$42,750
San Francisco, CA	$53,650

Average Earnings in Most Important Industries

Industry	Average Annual Earnings
Transportation Equipment Manufacturing	$57,020
Plastics and Rubber Products Manufacturing	$42,300
Machinery Manufacturing	$41,800
Fabricated Metal Product Manufacturing	$40,330
Primary Metal Manufacturing	$39,650

TOP EXECUTIVES

- Average Earnings: $91,347
- Beginning Earnings: $43,286
- 25th Percentile: $61,301
- 75th Percentile: $103,964

Average Earnings in Major Metropolitan Areas

Metropolitan Area	Average Annual Earnings
Atlanta, GA	$91,925
Chicago, IL	$98,469
Dallas-Fort Worth, TX	$93,761
Denver, CO	$98,286
Los Angeles, CA	$104,454
Minneapolis-St. Paul, MN	$97,493
New York, NY	$127,503
Phoenix, AZ	$88,501
San Francisco, CA	$111,073
Seattle, WA	$119,575

Average Earnings in Most Important Industries

Industry	Average Annual Earnings
Professional, Scientific, and Technical Services	$118,239
Merchant Wholesalers, Durable Goods	$98,718
Specialty Trade Contractors	$87,752
Administrative and Support Services	$83,692
Federal, State, and Local Government	$74,058

TRAVEL AGENTS

- Average Earnings: $28,670
- Beginning Earnings: $18,150
- 25th Percentile: $22,420
- 75th Percentile: $36,140

Average Earnings in Major Metropolitan Areas

Metropolitan Area	Average Annual Earnings
Atlanta, GA	$28,550
Chicago, IL	$25,430
Dallas-Fort Worth, TX	$32,240
Denver, CO	$27,670
Los Angeles, CA	$29,730
Minneapolis-St. Paul, MN	$35,570
New York, NY	$32,340
Phoenix, AZ	$25,870
San Francisco, CA	$33,390
Seattle, WA	$35,920

Average Earnings in Most Important Industries

Industry	Average Annual Earnings
Administrative and Support Services	$28,640

TRUCK DRIVERS AND DRIVER/SALES WORKERS

- Average Earnings: $29,362
- Beginning Earnings: $18,527
- 25th Percentile: $22,748
- 75th Percentile: $38,094

Average Earnings in Major Metropolitan Areas

Metropolitan Area	Average Annual Earnings
Atlanta, GA	$31,140
Chicago, IL	$35,646
Dallas-Fort Worth, TX	$29,534
Denver, CO	$31,175
Los Angeles, CA	$27,654
Minneapolis-St. Paul, MN	$32,323
New York, NY	$34,687
Phoenix, AZ	$29,675
San Francisco, CA	$32,737
Seattle, WA	$31,717

Average Earnings in Most Important Industries

Industry	Average Annual Earnings
Couriers and Messengers	$36,708
Truck Transportation	$35,543
Merchant Wholesalers, Nondurable Goods	$29,362
Merchant Wholesalers, Durable Goods	$26,200
Food Services and Drinking Places	$14,379

URBAN AND REGIONAL PLANNERS

- Average Earnings: $55,170
- Beginning Earnings: $34,920
- 25th Percentile: $43,360
- 75th Percentile: $69,490

Average Earnings in Major Metropolitan Areas

Metropolitan Area	Average Annual Earnings
Atlanta, GA	$51,840
Chicago, IL	$57,010
Dallas-Fort Worth, TX	$55,970
Denver, CO	$61,410
Los Angeles, CA	$68,050
Minneapolis-St. Paul, MN	$58,520
New York, NY	$64,390
Phoenix, AZ	$54,470
San Francisco, CA	$76,880
Seattle, WA	$66,080

Average Earnings in Most Important Industries

Industry	Average Annual Earnings
Professional, Scientific, and Technical Services	$61,070
Federal, State, and Local Government	$54,230

VETERINARIANS

- Average Earnings: $68,910
- Beginning Earnings: $40,960
- 25th Percentile: $53,550
- 75th Percentile: $90,760

Average Earnings in Major Metropolitan Areas

Metropolitan Area	Average Annual Earnings
Atlanta, GA	$55,390
Chicago, IL	$67,090
Dallas-Fort Worth, TX	$64,420
Denver, CO	$65,770
Los Angeles, CA	$86,290
Minneapolis-St. Paul, MN	$63,870
New York, NY	$89,680
Phoenix, AZ	$76,240
San Francisco, CA	$79,040
Seattle, WA	$79,340

Average Earnings in Most Important Industries

Industry	Average Annual Earnings
Professional, Scientific, and Technical Services	$68,840

VETERINARY TECHNOLOGISTS AND TECHNICIANS

- Average Earnings: $25,670
- Beginning Earnings: $17,700
- 25th Percentile: $20,870
- 75th Percentile: $31,560

Average Earnings in Major Metropolitan Areas

Metropolitan Area	Average Annual Earnings
Atlanta, GA	$25,770
Chicago, IL	$26,420
Dallas-Fort Worth, TX	$25,920
Denver, CO	$24,720
Los Angeles, CA	$28,100
Minneapolis-St. Paul, MN	$29,100
New York, NY	$28,900
Phoenix, AZ	$24,270
San Francisco, CA	$33,240
Seattle, WA	$32,460

Average Earnings in Most Important Industries

Industry	Average Annual Earnings
Professional, Scientific, and Technical Services	$25,350

WATER AND LIQUID WASTE TREATMENT PLANT AND SYSTEM OPERATORS

- Average Earnings: $34,930
- Beginning Earnings: $21,210
- 25th Percentile: $27,250
- 75th Percentile: $43,800

Average Earnings in Major Metropolitan Areas

Metropolitan Area	Average Annual Earnings
Atlanta, GA	$32,600
Chicago, IL	$42,450
Dallas-Fort Worth, TX	$32,820
Denver, CO	$46,850
Los Angeles, CA	$53,950
Minneapolis-St. Paul, MN	$42,400
Phoenix, AZ	$41,300
San Francisco, CA	$59,370
Seattle, WA	$50,950

Average Earnings in Most Important Industries

Industry	Average Annual Earnings
Chemical Manufacturing	$40,800
Federal, State, and Local Government	$35,000
Utilities	$34,410
Waste Management and Remediation Services	$34,950
Food Manufacturing	$29,050

WATER TRANSPORTATION OCCUPATIONS

- Average Earnings: $41,793
- Beginning Earnings: $24,769
- 25th Percentile: $31,388
- 75th Percentile: $54,984

Average Earnings in Major Metropolitan Areas

Metropolitan Area	Average Annual Earnings
Chicago, IL	$24,230
Los Angeles, CA	$35,870
Minneapolis-St. Paul, MN	$40,090
New York, NY	$51,223
San Francisco, CA	$46,390
Seattle, WA	$51,239

Average Earnings in Most Important Industries

Industry	Average Annual Earnings
Water Transportation	$44,124
Support Activities for Transportation	$44,282
Federal, State, and Local Government	$44,383
Rental and Leasing Services	$38,618
Scenic and Sightseeing Transportation	$30,041

WEIGHERS, MEASURERS, CHECKERS, AND SAMPLERS, RECORDKEEPING

- Average Earnings: $25,310
- Beginning Earnings: $16,410
- 25th Percentile: $19,930
- 75th Percentile: $32,890

Average Earnings in Major Metropolitan Areas

Metropolitan Area	Average Annual Earnings
Atlanta, GA	$25,170
Chicago, IL	$26,550
Dallas-Fort Worth, TX	$26,120
Denver, CO	$31,230
Los Angeles, CA	$22,910
Minneapolis-St. Paul, MN	$33,720
New York, NY	$28,630
Phoenix, AZ	$31,610
San Francisco, CA	$28,470
Seattle, WA	$34,300

Average Earnings in Most Important Industries

Industry	Average Annual Earnings
Food and Beverage Stores	$27,260
Merchant Wholesalers, Nondurable Goods	$25,290
Merchant Wholesalers, Durable Goods	$25,080
Food Manufacturing	$23,650
Administrative and Support Services	$22,330

WELDING, SOLDERING, AND BRAZING WORKERS

- Average Earnings: $30,927
- Beginning Earnings: $20,419
- 25th Percentile: $24,927
- 75th Percentile: $37,906

Average Earnings in Major Metropolitan Areas

Metropolitan Area	Average Annual Earnings
Atlanta, GA	$28,820
Chicago, IL	$32,663
Dallas-Fort Worth, TX	$27,982
Denver, CO	$32,586
Los Angeles, CA	$26,753
Minneapolis-St. Paul, MN	$38,447
New York, NY	$32,535
Phoenix, AZ	$29,040
San Francisco, CA	$41,020
Seattle, WA	$39,666

Average Earnings in Most Important Industries

Industry	Average Annual Earnings
Specialty Trade Contractors	$32,911
Transportation Equipment Manufacturing	$32,088
Machinery Manufacturing	$30,877
Fabricated Metal Product Manufacturing	$29,783
Merchant Wholesalers, Durable Goods	$29,297

WOODWORKERS

- Average Earnings: $24,457
- Beginning Earnings: $16,366
- 25th Percentile: $19,652
- 75th Percentile: $30,686

Average Earnings in Major Metropolitan Areas

Metropolitan Area	Average Annual Earnings
Atlanta, GA	$24,403
Chicago, IL	$35,051
Dallas-Fort Worth, TX	$21,122
Denver, CO	$28,834
Los Angeles, CA	$21,631
Minneapolis-St. Paul, MN	$33,419
New York, NY	$31,279
Phoenix, AZ	$22,670
San Francisco, CA	$31,221
Seattle, WA	$28,697

Average Earnings in Most Important Industries

Industry	Average Annual Earnings
Furniture and Related Product Manufacturing	$24,997
Wood Product Manufacturing	$23,254

WRITERS AND EDITORS

- Average Earnings: $48,126
- Beginning Earnings: $27,890
- 25th Percentile: $36,158
- 75th Percentile: $65,250

Average Earnings in Major Metropolitan Areas

Metropolitan Area	Average Annual Earnings
Atlanta, GA	$52,890
Chicago, IL	$45,704
Dallas-Fort Worth, TX	$50,359
Denver, CO	$52,617
Los Angeles, CA	$54,223
Minneapolis-St. Paul, MN	$48,287
New York, NY	$59,081
Phoenix, AZ	$39,561
San Francisco, CA	$62,965
Seattle, WA	$65,457

Average Earnings in Most Important Industries

Industry	Average Annual Earnings
Professional, Scientific, and Technical Services	$51,938
Religious, Grantmaking, Civic, Professional, and Similar Organizations	$48,750
Publishing Industries (Except Internet)	$45,045
Broadcasting (Except Internet)	$43,436
Educational Services	$43,399

Compensation and Benefits Analysis Worksheet

The following worksheet encompasses the major aspects of compensation and benefits. You can use it to estimate and assess the total compensation package of your current or former position, as well as that of the new position you are being offered. Quantifying the variables in this way will help you decide which parts of the offer are financially acceptable, and which parts you will want to negotiate. You can also use the worksheet to evaluate one job offer against another.

Not all of the following benefits are linked in every instance to a direct financial reward, but they may add to the quality of work and/or personal life.

SALARY AND BONUS

Benefit	Description	Current Job Employee Cost/Dollar Value	Job Offer #1 Employee Cost/Dollar Value	Job Offer #2 Employee Cost/Dollar Value
Base salary/wages				
Short-term incentives				
Long-term incentives				
Equity ownership				

HEALTH CARE

Benefit	Description	Current Job Employee Cost/Dollar Value	Job Offer #1 Employee Cost/Dollar Value	Job Offer #2 Employee Cost/Dollar Value
Medical insurance				
Dental/other insurance				
Prescription drug coverage				
Health-care spending account				
Wellness programs				

INCOME PROTECTION

Benefit	Description	Current Job Employee Cost/Dollar Value	Job Offer #1 Employee Cost/Dollar Value	Job Offer #2 Employee Cost/Dollar Value
Sick pay				
Short- and long-term disability insurance				
Life insurance				
Extended/other financial insurance coverage				
Business liability insurance				

RETIREMENT

Benefit	Description	Current Job Employee Cost/Dollar Value	Job Offer #1 Employee Cost/Dollar Value	Job Offer #2 Employee Cost/Dollar Value
Defined-benefit pension plan				
Defined-contribution plan				
Stock/stock options				
Portability of retirement funds				

RELOCATION

Benefit	Description	Current Job Employee Cost/Dollar Value	Job Offer #1 Employee Cost/Dollar Value	Job Offer #2 Employee Cost/Dollar Value
Lump-sum expense reimbursement				
Assistance with sale of existing home				
House-hunting allowance				
Moving expenses				
New home purchase assistance				

WORK/LIFE BALANCE

Benefit	Description	Current Job Employee Cost/Dollar Value	Job Offer #1 Employee Cost/Dollar Value	Job Offer #2 Employee Cost/Dollar Value
Schedule and location flexibility				
Paid time off				
Time off without pay				
Meals				
Parking				

WORK/LIFE BALANCE (CONTINUED)

Benefit	Description	Current Job Employee Cost/Dollar Value	Job Offer #1 Employee Cost/Dollar Value	Job Offer #2 Employee Cost/Dollar Value
Commuter assistance				
Career development and education reimbursement				
Lifestyle management and employee assistance				
Family and dependent care support				
Financial and legal assistance				

BUSINESS ENTERTAINMENT AND TRAVEL

Benefit	Description	Current Job Employee Cost/Dollar Value	Job Offer #1 Employee Cost/Dollar Value	Job Offer #2 Employee Cost/Dollar Value
Business entertainment reimbursement				
Company car				
Business travel expense reimbursement				
Other entertainment and travel benefits				

EXECUTIVE AND SUPPLEMENTAL BENEFITS

Benefit	Description	Current Job Employee Cost/Dollar Value	Job Offer #1 Employee Cost/Dollar Value	Job Offer #2 Employee Cost/Dollar Value
Enhanced offer packages				
Executive equity ownership plan				
Long-term cash incentives or equity				
Deferred compensation/ SERP				
Supplemental insurance				

Index